"If you want the
present to be different from the past,
study the past."

Baruch  Spinoza

# Contents

# 1

## *Aunt Amelia's Jewish Stories*

*T*he twenty-three came off the boat penniless with only the shirts on their backs. Pirates attacked and robbed them on the way. You really want to hear more?" asked Aunt Amelia. "Aren't you tired yet? You've heard my stories since you were a little girl."

Emma grinned and shook her head. "You tell the most magical stories. What I like most about them is that they really, really happened."

Her aunt laughed. "Oh, yes. Only God knows how these men did that."

"Did what?" she asked eagerly. "Oh, tell us Auntie Amelia, please, please, please."

Aunt Amelia was a great favorite not only of Emma's but her siblings as well. They were Sarah, Josephine, Mary, Agnes, Frank Eliezer (the only boy) and Annie, the youngest of the girls.

"Well then, I'll tell you about the first twenty-three Jews who came to New York harbor."

"The Sepharadim?" asked Emma.

"Yes. They emerged after an amazing adventure way back on the seventh day of September 1654. Actually, at the time, they called themselves 'of the Portuguese nation.'"

"Weren't they members of ancient noble families?" asked Josephine, one of the older sisters.

"Oh, yes. They were philosophers, physicians, judges, astronomers and advisors to kings during Spain's most glorious moments. They had enjoyed the trust and friendship of the royal families."

"So what happened next?" asked Emma. "How did they get here?"

"It was a risky voyage. None of them could have envisioned the surprise that would happen at sea. Pirates attacked and robbed them. When they got off the boat, they set up a camp of sorts on the banks of the Hudson. After an ordeal of nearly two months there, these settlers who had inadvertently become America's first minority group were free, or at least somewhat free to making a living."

Emma nodded gravely. "Were they our relatives?" she asked.

"Yes, we're connected," Aunt Amelia replied.

"So, are some of them, I mean their children's, children's children, I mean these relatives, are they still poor today?" Emma's eyes became wide open.

"No, no. They soon prospered again as they'd done earlier in Spain and Portugal. My darlings, you know that our families are known as the aristocrats among Jews."

Josephine and Sarah nodded.

"Hum," said Emma. She was certainly happy to hear that especially due to her plans to dress up as Queen Esther, for the upcoming Purim party.

## 2

## *Purim Fun*

*M*rs. Lazarus was busy in her spacious kitchen. It was time to get the little packages ready to exchange with family and friends. She was looking at the handsome Homentashen her housekeeper had baked in the morning, and it made her heart sing. All she had to do now was put the pastries in baskets, add some fruit, tie them up neatly with blue ribbons and they would be done.

"Moses," Mrs. Lazarus called to Emma's father, "have you seen Albert this afternoon?"

"I haven't been anywhere near the Knickerbockers Club today. Aren't you proud of your cousin now that he's been appointed Justice of the Supreme Court of the State of New York?"

"Yes, I am. Justice Cardozo sounds good. I thought you liked the Club, so how come...?"

"Well, today the new equipment's coming in. I had to check that it does everything they said it did. You know how it is."

"And...?"

Moses grinned. "It may just speed things up a bit."

"That's marvelous, isn't it?'

"It looks like these machines will more than double the refining of our sugar. No one has seen anything like that."

"That's no surprise to me. I know that you're a smart businessman," she said, tying another blue ribbon around a basket. "In fact, everyone else in town knows that."

Frank, Emma's younger brother, hopped around in the living room dressed up as a frog. The girls decided to dress up as clowns except Emma. She was Queen Esther.

Mr. Lazarus roared with delight, "My, oh my, a prettier Queen I've never seen."

Emma loved to see her father laugh. She stood still, enjoying each chuckle. Holding his sides, Moses gasped for breath, "Esther, we'd better be on our way to the synagogue or we'll miss the reading of the Megilla."

Sherit Israel was the first synagogue in New York City. When the Lazarus family walked in, the atmosphere was festive and joyful. All the Purim decorations were moving colorfully through the air: the balloons, the masks, and the paper chains. Candlelight glowed from the center table. Men, women, old and young, held on to their noisemakers (better known as graggers) in one hand and masks with the other. Men reading the Megilla in familiar tunes heartily and reverently where often joined by their congregates.

From the aisle, a little boy began singing in a high sweet voice, "Purim, Purim all year round, all year round."

Suddenly everyone spun their graggers when Haman's name was mentioned. He was the villain of the Purim story, the meanest of the mean. The barrage of noise was to drown out his name and erase it from the face of the earth.

"Too bad the service is in Hebrew," Emma thought. "Father can understand it," she said proudly to her mother.

"Perhaps one day I will too," she thought, "but may be not." After the reading there was the Purim play.

Emma and her siblings knew the story, about the Persian King who'd married Esther, the orphan Jewish girl, who was very pretty and wise. Her dearest cousin, Mordecai, would often come by to see her in the palace. On one of these visits, he overheard that there was a plot to kill the king. He quickly told Esther to inform her husband and so the king was saved.

Emma leaned forward as Haman and his wife walked onto the stage. She stared out toward the actors and smiled when he said to his wife: "You know, Mordecai, the Jew, annoys the heck out of me." Haman looked funny with his triangular hat and everybody in the audience burst out laughing.

"Why is that, your Lordship?" his wife asked.

"He refuses to bow down to me! That's no way to treat the most powerful minister in the entire kingdom."

"That's right, my husband, my Lord."

"I'll teach him a lesson. I'll have the king order to kill him and all the Jews in the kingdom."

"Crush them, my Lordship!"

"I'll have all the power in all of Persia and no one will be left to disobey me."

The scene changed. This time Mordecai and Esther were near the palace. Emma sat up to listen carefully as Mordecai said, "Esther darling, I need your help. You must do something to prevent a tragedy."

"What's wrong?"

"If we don't act quickly our people will be annihilated. Haman has permission to kill all the Jews. Esther, sweetheart, you must talk to the king. You must stop Haman from acting out his craziness."

"But I can't go to the king unless I'm invited. I'm not allowed to walk in on him whenever I feel like it."

"Listen, this time is different, I beg you. Do your best, be your best and look your best."

"But I'm scared. I'm afraid I can't."

"Esther, how do you know that God hasn't placed you in the palace for just this moment to intervene and save your people?"

Emma sensed a hush. No one in the audience moved, but something Mordecai had said stirred Emma's heart. As the story played out, that question challenged and emboldened Esther to go to the king and, by so doing, rescue the lives of innocent people.

After the round of applause, there was dancing and prizes.

"It's time for us to go home," Mrs. Lazarus said, sounding reluctant.

"Already?" said Emma, slightly jolting her shoulders.

As always, when she was interested, she wanted to stay longer not to miss anything.

Their beautiful apartment looked warm and comfortable. The joyful singing and laughter filled the air. Emma was at the piano with all the family gathered around. Her sweet voice joined in with those of her sisters and her father's rich tenor.

"There was a message about Purim from Rabbi Gershon Seixas in the paper tonight," Mrs. Lazarus remarked. "He said what we all feel, I think. Why not read it to us, Josephine. Reading aloud is good practice."

Her father settled down comfortably in a big chair. Josephine picked up the paper, found her place and read the headline slowly, with understanding, "A tug of war between good and evil. Purim is a holiday of liberation."

Then she proceeded to read the rest of it, "Esther was comfortable in the royal palace and she wanted to live a quiet, happy life as a queen. Suddenly she needs to cope with a frightening decision. But Mordecai's message is clear. Esther must act or she and many innocent people will die.

By her action she changes the course of history, making it fitting that the book be named for her."

"Well done, Josephine, and well done Rabbi Gershon Seixas. I didn't think your Uncle had it in him to be so articulate," Mr. Lazarus said.

"Hey, Mother, your name is also Esther. Then it's your book, too," said Emma excitedly.

Mrs. Lazarus smiled calmly and the girls chuckled.

"Bedtime now," said Mrs. Lazarus cheerfully. "Give your father a good night kiss and off to bed with you children."

Like many wealthy New Yorkers, Moses had a charming wife and a delightful family. His personal wealth was very substantial. His political connections had been enough to open any door. He had three powerful assets: a family fortune, a family tree and a love for learning. He wanted to give his children all three of them.

# 3

# Brave Fighters

Mr. Lazarus was at the head of the table as usual, and Mrs. Lazarus at the other end with Annie's high chair next to her. Agnes, Mary and Sarah sat on the side and Josephine, Emma and Frank on the other side. Mr. Lazarus' face was grim. "Newspapers are writing terrible things about the war. It's brutal."

Esther only shook her head, her lips forming a tight line. Sarah mentioned that her friend had seen young men in dusty, torn blue uniforms getting off the train. Some were bandaged, some used crutches. She saw trainloads of them.

"Surely you can't say they ran away from anything they thought was their duty," exclaimed Mrs. Lazarus.

"It sounds," said Mr. Lazarus "like some had to ride at breakneck speed to escape the enemy." His calm hazel eyes met her dark eyes, and Emma understood that her mother and father were discussing a grave matter.

Emma was only eleven when the Civil War broke out. She couldn't help hearing a great deal about it. Grown-ups talked of little else. Some were angry when they read, "The soldiers were riddled with bullets when they were crossing a bridge that was being shelled."

Mothers worried about their sons being so close to the front, their faces black with the smoke of powder under enemy fire. Stories were told and Emma listened intently. Her dark eyes were as bright as ever when she heard her mother talk with a cousin. "The army hospitals are too far from the battle fields. Many men died on the way before they received treatment."

"Some orderlies were moving with difficulty in the mud at Palmouth looking for wounded men," added Mrs. Lazarus.

"The problem is," chimed in Josephine, "they were not ready to take better care of the soldiers who were wounded."

Mrs. Lazarus sighed softly, "Yes, that's what I've been hearing. They don't have enough aid stations."

Small and slender, Emma was upset hearing about all the men who'd died. She knew this time the trouble was not in far lands and in distant times; it was close to home. She seemed to understand the hardship of war in spite of her tender years.

One morning when she looked out her window, she was taken by the brilliance of gold leaves against the blue sky. The earth looked fresh after the storm. The door to the bathroom was open and the yellow soap was rich with the scent of lemon and orange blossoms. Emma felt her own heart full of a song she wanted to let out. She found a sheet of paper and sat down in the quiet corner at her desk. Words flowed in her mind and she scribbled them down as fast as she could:

"One by one the summer flowers are now dying...
I cried all my soul in the cry,
To the mountains, and the woods,
And the gold tinted sky,
I am sad. I am weary of all this world's strife."

It took only a few minutes to finish ten lines. She ran with the poem to the living room, to her father, who was resting in his comfortable chair.

15

"Listen, Papa!" She read it aloud.

Moses rubbed his chin thoughtfully. "Well done, Emma!" he exclaimed.

"That's lovely," added Mrs. Lazarus.

Josephine and Sarah and Agnes crowded around to read it again for themselves. "Doesn't she look like an angel?" asked Sarah.

"She certainly charms all of us with her golden tongue and quick mind," said Josephine.

Agnes gave her a hug and said, "Emma, you're a born singer."

"Why, thank you." Emma thought. She had never been so happy before in her life. In fact, she also loved music, and when she played the piano, her imagination was like a magic carpet. She loved the music lessons, but she didn't care to practice. Emma often said, "I don't like playing the same thing over and over again. I get tired."

No one could force her. Yet her teacher found a way when he said, "All right then, unless you know your lesson, we can't move on to the next piece." That bothered Emma because she was curious and filled with pleasure when she learned something new. Reading was another one of her favorite things to do.

After she'd taken several brisk turns about the room, Mr. Lazarus seemed to suspect that something was brewing in his little girl's mind. "What's this book that you're holding?"

"Papa, it's about Judah the Maccabi. I love it."

"Why do you like it that much?"

"It's the Hanukkah story. It tells how the brave Maccabim fought the strong Syrian army who'd invaded Jerusalem."

"Oh, that's an astounding story. With a lot of lucky breaks, they won the battle. They drove the Syrians out of their land and regained freedom and independence. It's pretty amazing how they could pinpoint something exactly with bow and arrow and strike at the strong enemy."

"What I liked most about the Maccabim is their courage. Even though they were few and the Syrians were many and strong. And I especially like the story about the oil and the light that lasted for eight days."

Mr. Lazarus made sure that his children would remember that the lesson of Hanukkah was to bring light into places of darkness. That's why when Emma was growing up, her father used to kindle an additional candle each evening for eight days of the holiday.

# 4

# No School

"Time to get up!"

"Em, Mother." Emma rolled over.

Her bed was covered with a pink quilt. It was as light as a marshmallow and very warm. She curled up, and it seemed that Emma didn't want to leave her bed. She closed her eyes again. Emma liked to stay in her dream world, half asleep and half awake; these were delicious moments. But then she didn't want her mother to think that she was sick so she jumped out of bed in a hurry.

Some days though, Emma's energy was low, and she was not strong enough to go to school. That's why she was tutored at home.

"My, my!" Mrs. Lazarus said. "What a hurry you're in this morning!"

Emma grinned. She knew what her mother meant. She had a lot of memorizing to do, and she was proudest when she recited beautiful lines from her favorite poets.

The Lazarus' sat down to breakfast. It was a hearty breakfast, too. The pancakes were delicious and Emma ate hungrily. "Don't forget, Mother," Emma cried. "You promised I could have pecan pie."

Mrs. Lazarus laughed, "You'll get your pecan pie, Emma. Everybody will get to pick the cake they want at teatime."

"What a fine day it is," said Moses, as he looked out the window. "Too nice a day, for a girl to stay inside."

Emma shook her head vigorously. She liked sunshine and blue skies, but she would rather read. Frank couldn't wait to take out his bike and go for a ride. Josephine and Sarah suggested Emma join them for a walk. Emma, however, showed no interest.

"Well, let me say this much for Emma, she would rather stay cooped up in her room," said Josephine.

"I bet she would rather read her amazing Greek stories about the Greek gods and goddesses. The girl's a thinker. Every now and then I catch her lost in thought." Moses winked at Emma.

"I believe a 'dreamer' is the word people use," said Josephine.

For the most part though, Emma enjoyed her lessons at home. Mr. Lazarus and Emma always seemed to be having a good time. They would laugh as they studied. She asked many questions, and he was glad. "That is the best way for children to learn," he would say.

Two girls often came up to the Lazarus' home. They were Rose Hawthorne and Minnie Biddle. Those two had become Emma's very good friends. Rose was her best friend; she was the daughter of the famous author Nathaniel Hawthorne. More often though, Emma was too busy to spend a whole lot of time with them, her interests were many: literature, history and mythology. She had a gift for languages and took up French, Italian and German, even trying her hand at translating poems into English.

After reading the Greek stories, she loved stomping around the center of the parlor, her "stage," making believe she was Venus, the golden–haired goddess of love rising from the sea.

In an outburst of joy, she scribbled down quickly.

"'Tis good to be alive,
And why?
Simply,
To see the light,
That plays upon the grass,"

Emma derived great enjoyment from reading her favorite authors. She loved George Eliot, Charles Dickens, the French Victor Hugo and German Heine and Goethe, as well as, Walter Scott's historical novels, such as Ivanhoe. She especially was interested in the stories about how difficult it was for families trying to make a life in a new place. She often wondered, "What if I had been born in another country? What would she have been like in a new place? What was it like to be poor?"

In her chronicles, besides making references, she commented, "Although I don't go to school, I certainly have fun at home. Still, how could I do otherwise with a lovely family like mine?"

"Emma, Mother is calling, did you hear?" Josephine walked into her room.

"Why, no!" Emma looked at her sister in astonishment,

"I'm sorry, I didn't hear a thing."

"I believe you," said Josephine. "Come along now, before supper gets cold."

Emma closed her diary with a snap and went along. Over dinner, Emma told everyone who was willing to listen about her history class. "It's our history that holds us together, particularly the revolution and what we believe in."

"You couldn't study a more interesting subject," said Mr. Lazarus. "History is not what everybody thinks. What I mean is everybody thinks crisis situations are the result of just one bad decision."

"No?" Josephine was surprised.

"No, no. I agree. My tutor said the exact same thing. He said that our situation today is not the result of just one single choice," Josephine continued.

"That's right," said Mr. Lazarus. "People start down a particular road, then they take another little step, and another. That's why it's also fair to say that 'the future is now.'"

"You mean that we are creating it now by the choices we make?" asked Emma.

Mr. Lazarus nodded his head in agreement and his eyelids went up and down at the same time. "You got it," he said.

The moon was full that night, and Emma saw it from her bedroom window as she put on a pink silky nightgown. She thought of all the little quibbles she had with Josephine or hadn't minded her mother or was cross with Frank the prankster. It made her sad. Emma couldn't hold back her tears. After crying her heart out, she felt much better. She climbed into bed, pulled the covers up and began to recite to herself a little bedtime prayer, "Hear oh, Israel,..."

# 5

## Bread with No Taste

*H*ere was the most exciting thing about today: the whole family would celebrate Passover. Mr. Lazarus was not a religious man, but family traditions were important to the Lazarus', and a Seder was part of the proud history of his ancestors.

Several days of unusually mild weather ushered in a splendid spring. Budding trees and warm temperatures had replaced the snow and ice and biting cold. The girls were all excited about this special evening. To begin with, Grandpa and Grandma were to arrive early. Then, Mrs. Lazarus was in an uncommonly outgoing mood that morning, unlike her usual calm manner.

"You're going to ask the four questions, Frankie," Emma teased her little brother. Frank moved his fingers towards Emma's head and looked like he was about to pull his sister's hair for bringing that up. Instead, he stuck his tongue out at her behind Mr. Lazarus' back.

"Agnes," called Mrs. Lazarus, "put the matza on the table. Make sure it's in the center."

Then she called out again, "Emma, can you help me get the Seder-plate ready?"

Emma was eager to get into the kitchen and see all the baked goodies. They were very special because none of these delicacies had any flour in them.

"Father, what are you looking for?" asked Josephine.

"Now, where did I put all the Haggaddas?"

"Why do we need them, anyway? You seem to know it by heart. Why don't we just go ahead and eat?" asked Frank as he made a face at Josephine that was half a wink.

"Well, 'Seder' means 'order' in Hebrew. Tonight, there is a special order to everything we do at the table. The book we call Hagaddah tells us exactly how to proceed in telling the story of our people," said Mr. Lazarus.

"The time they were slaves in Egypt some three- thousand years ago. Papa, haven't you told us this same story last year and the year before that, and before that?" asked Frank.

Mr. Lazarus looked at his son and smiled.

Emma brought in the Seder - plate and put it on the table.

"Actually, you can tell the story of Passover just by looking at the plate," Frank chuckled.

"I'm not so sure," protested Josephine. "It's true, that the 'shank bone' represents the Passover lamb which stands for freedom. And the 'bitter herbs' remind us of slavery. But still the main food of Passover is matza, it's key to our celebration."

"Yes, the bread with no taste," said Emma.

"Well, what do you expect? It has no salt and no spices. It's the most primitive form of bread. That's what the slaves ate," said Josephine.

"I believe," said Emma, "that the foods are our way of personally taking part in the exodus from Egypt. It's kind of acting out the story of when we were slaves and how we became free." As she said this, a vague memory crossed her mind, something to do with her father's business partner. She thought she'd heard he owned slaves in the South. Emma understood her father didn't like that about his partner so she didn't want to bring it up.

"Want to know the part I like most?" Mrs. Lazarus called out from the kitchen. "Tonight your father becomes a king and your mother a queen. Isn't that right, Moses?"

The girls hooted with laughter. Frank rolled his eyes and stood there with his mouth open.

"That's right," Moses confirmed as he stooped to face Esther turning again to look for the Hagaddas. "Here they are, I found them. Now, let's get started."

Everything was ready. Fragile porcelain plated and tea cups along with finest glassware and antique silver spoons decorated the table." Everybody took their seats. Moses filled the cups with red wine.

"We do this every year over and over, again and again."

"Frank," said Mrs. Lazarus, "you weren't even around for that many Seders."

"Still..." said Frank a little bashfully.

"Well," said Mr. Lazarus, "it's a story of freedom and hope. Besides, Jewish law commands us to 'tell it to your child.' To make sure we remember who we are and where we came from."

Moses began chanting, "This is the bread of suffering which our ancestors ate in the land of Egypt. Let all who are hungry come and eat. Let all who are needy come..."

After some more reading, everybody took their turn at dipping a piece of parsley in salt water. The salt water was for the tears of the slaves and the parsley represented spring, hope and renewal.

Emma noticed the pictures of the ten plagues distracted Frank. She gave him a jolt and giggled when he raised his head suddenly and looked at his father as he kept spilling drops of wine each time he mentioned a plague.

"I suppose each time we lose drops of wine, we lose some joy. Father, that's what you told us last year."

"And that teaches us what?" Mr. Lazarus expected her to finish the sentence.

"To have compassion for the Egyptians." Emma was proud that she actually remembered the small details.

Mr. Lazarus turned to his daughters, his deep eyes gazing into theirs, were very dark. "My girls want to please me on this special day, don't you?"

Each of them began reading their parts and then they all sang together.

"Are we going to eat now?" asked Frank.

And yes, this time it was time to eat. Emma could smell the desserts even though they were still in the kitchen; she liked the sugary aroma.

"Esther, that was delicious," said Moses.

"I'm stuffed," said Emma. Frank tapped his tummy.

"Now, we need the Afikoman." Mr. Lazarus smiled and moved his head from side to side indicating that he'd hoped that someone would find the matza he'd hidden away. He wanted to give the young folks an opportunity to go "matza hunting" and give it to him once they discover the hiding place.

"That's the best part of the Seder," said Frank, all excited and rubbing his hands together. "I like it when we get to negotiate the gifts we want in exchange for the Afikoman."

"You bet," said all his siblings almost in chorus.

Mr. Lazarus was a loving father and a beloved man.

He was often very generous with his gifts. Emma laughed when she saw Frank jump up and down as he spotted the coming of his little presents. The real gifts, though, all of them would expect to get, would arrive no sooner than in a week or two.

Then, Mrs. Lazarus suddenly called out, "Would somebody go and open the door for Elijah, please?"

Frank jumped off his chair and tumbled over a stool. His face was full of suppressed excitement and his voice so joyful that everybody perked up. He ran to the door and said in a breathless voice, "Here he comes..."

"I bet no one really knows why Elijah gets the biggest goblet of wine," Sarah said with a smirk.

"This mysteriously invisible man," said Mr. Lazarus, "is visiting all the Jewish families this evening and he brings hope for all those who are in despair."

"How come he is a prophet of such great good news?" asked Emma.

Mrs. Lazarus moved the goblet a little more to the center. She was careful not to spill the wine.

"Well," said Mr. Lazarus, "to begin with, his death was spectacular. Actually, he never died. As the story goes, he was walking with his successor, Elisha, when there appeared a chariot and horses of fire and separated between the two of them. Then suddenly, Elijah went up in a whirlwind into heaven."

"Hey, that's a neat story," said Emma, "and here comes my favorite song."

"Mine, too," Josephine agreed. "You mean Had Gadia?"

"Yes," said Emma in a high-pitched tone. "It has such a silly ring to it, it's all about that goat and the cat and the fire and the water..."

Grandma Sarah joined in the conversation with a question of her own. "I always puzzled over that. Why would we end the Seder with a song about a goat?"

Mr. Lazarus laughed, but then he seized the opportunity to teach his children to be better people and he said, "That is to show how everything is connected to everything else. And how the behavior of one, can affect everybody."

Then the Lazarus family concluded the Seder by reading the last part together, "next year in Jerusalem and let people everywhere be free."

"I'm so full of happiness," said Grandma Sarah sighing with contentment as she sat down in the study to rest after the excitement and to refresh herself from the festive meal. Now the Lazarus family, and the Jews world over, had a little challenge ahead of them: no bread for the next seven days, except matza.

# 6

## Emma's Surprise

*E*mma was so fond of writing that most of the time the second finger of her right hand was inky. "I have heaps to tell," she scribbled in her diary. "Friday was a great day. Father brought us our gifts and stirred up a lot of commotion. Frankie got his box of figurines, and I got a beautiful silk scarf. I love the pattern; it seems to be Japanese. Josephine got her Shakespeare that was many books in one. Father told her, "Read him well and he will help you understand the study of character."

"It sounds like something I could use to understand people a whole lot better, Tom for one," Emma sighed. "I don't quite know what he's really thinking of me. And, Mother is another story. She often says stuff between the lines and most of the time I don't get it." Emma corked up her inkstand and determined that would be enough for today.

She had great hopes for herself so she wrote constantly. To be an artist was the highest calling, a gift from the gods. Emma wrote poems about love and friendship and family holidays. In one of her poems she said,

"And I saw the great waters rise and fall,
Then I saw at last ... a golden and mystic ring.
But it floated near, it is love, oh welcome...
And I saw it was but
A yellow weed of the sea...
And it drifted away from me."

Like many teenage girls, Emma longed for romance. In her journal she wrote, "I have something to confess to you today. It is difficult to tell you because it is about myself. You are the best one to confide in because you'll always keep a secret. I get the feeling lately of being embarrassed and blush very easily. I wish I could stop getting all red like that. I've been trying to think of an excuse to say something to Tom and get him talking without it being noticeable, and my chance came yesterday. It gave me a queer feeling though, each time I looked into his eyes. But the evening passed and nothing happened. In fact, I don't think that I want it to be otherwise. I don't believe that he is 'it' for me."

Emma was too much of a free spirit to settle just for anybody. Besides, her real passion was elsewhere. She was set on becoming a "real poet." The stories of ancient gods of Greece captured her imagination and Pegasus, the steed of inspiration, especially enchanted her. He was considered to be the poet's greatest source of poetry.

His story set her on fire, and in her dreams, she often saw herself riding that winged horse. And in her daydreams, she hoped to win his love and soar with him through the mountains across the green meadows and let him cause poems to flow out of her heart.

When Emma was seventeen, a porter rang their doorbell. Mr. Lazarus was more than happy to see him. "Oh, here you are, that's what I've been waiting for. Thank you, thank you very much."

As the large carton was dropped off in the hallway, Emma wondered what was in that box? But then she figured it had something to do with her father's business. She went into the kitchen to have some silly fun with her little sister, Annie. In the meantime, Moses unpacked the carton and handed a few books at a time to Mrs. Lazarus.

"Aren't these handsome?" said Mrs. Lazarus.

"Yes, I believe the printer has done a fine job." Emma overheard her mother's voice as she walked out of the kitchen.

"Wait and see when she finds out." Moses smiled.

"Our girl will be in seventh heaven," said Mrs. Lazarus with a chuckle. Emma thought she'd heard her father say, "our girls." He liked to surprise them with gifts so she did not suspect that something very unusual was just about to happen.

After supper, Esther looked at Moses, and by her look, he figured now was the time. "Somebody is going to be very happy tonight," said Mr. Lazarus.

"Actually, we should all be happy. What's good for one of us is good for all of us. Isn't that so?" commented Mrs. Lazarus.

"Yes, Mother, so what is it?" asked Josephine.

Mr. Lazarus pulled out a book and said, "Emma dear, here's the fruit of your efforts, your mother and I are very proud of you." He kissed her on the cheek and handed it to her. Emma took one glance at the book and could not believe her eyes. It said *Poems and Translations by Emma Lazarus*. Moses had collected all her poems and had them printed to give as gifts to family and friends.

"Is it my book?" Emma exclaimed. When she held the book in her hands, it moved her so and she thought, "Was I really able to do this? How did I do it?" She looked at the book and looked at everybody at the table intermittently, she smiled and laughed. She was almost speechless. Emma didn't know how to thank her mother and father for that very unusual gift.

The girls cheered and Frank got up and applauded.

"I just hope that you're not going to show off too much after all that fuss," he said with a smirk.

Emma laughed and gave him a hug. She could hardly sleep that night. Over and over, she read her translation to Heine's poem from German,

"My heart is like a sun
So flaming and so light,
In a sea of love so deep."

Then she turned a few more pages and noticed her own poem.

"Let us love! Be two!
The two eyes make the face;
The two wings make the lark."

Emma had had some teenage crushes and felt the pain and disappointment they inflicted on a young girl's heart. She had better luck, though, with writing. Seeing her name on the cover of a book brought her joy, and it was a kind of "proof" that she was a poet, for real.

Now she was determined to work even harder. After all, she could not disappoint her father. When morning came, Emma's room was very still, but a bird sang cheerfully on a budding branch close by and the sun shined in like a blessing over the peaceful face on the pillow.

# 7

## *Party Talk*

*A*lthough their personalities were very different, it turned out that Emma and Tom Ward shared many interests. For starters, they both loved poetry and literature. As a result, they became good friends. He frequently visited their home on 36 West 14th Street and enjoyed evenings with the Lazarus family.

Late in 1866, Tom's father, Samuel G. Ward, gave a party for a childhood friend of his who'd come in from Concord. Emma was among the close circle of friends to be invited. When she walked into Samuel Ward's house, she was impressed by the merry sounds overflowing with happy faces and eyes smiling from every corner.

Emma overheard a young woman saying, "I don't really know. He might have a chance. He's been governor. That's always a good stepping stone to the White House."

"But the..."

The young men wore traditional black dress coats and high-standing collars with a broad opening giving them a look of dignity. Emma had on a long gown made of blue silk, tightly fitted around her thin waistline and a gardenia corsage.

The folding doors were thrown open revealing marble-topped tables piled high with turkey, mutton, pies and rich plum cake. Long mirrors and lace curtains in the parlor added to the special atmosphere of the evening. Emma greeted people she knew and exchanged some small talk.

Mrs. Ward was more than happy to see her. She took her hand, "Emma, darling, let me introduce you to our honored guest," she said cheerfully. Together they walked over to a tall, lean man who was old enough to be Emma's father.

"Ralph, please meet Emma. This fine young lady is very talented."

Mr. Emerson looked at Emma with his intensely blue eyes. His manner was serene. She smiled sweetly while at the same time her heart skipped a beat. She sensed a whole world was opening up for her. She knew it in her bones, in her inner excitement.

Emerson was a famous writer and philosopher. People respected and admired his words of wisdom. That's why some even called him "The Sage from Concord."

Thanks to her manners and quick mind, Emma was terrific with words. Most of the time she said just the right thing. In the course of her conversation with Emerson, she mentioned her family lived one block west of Union Square.

Mr. Emerson responded, "Hum, ha, that's the hub of activity isn't it?" rubbing his hair.

Emma laughed. "It sure is," she said. "New York has become a meeting place for writers and thinkers from all over. I feel truly fortunate to live here."

The evening was filled with music, both vocal and piano, to enhance the pleasure of the occasion. Emma was endowed with the gift of fascination, and Emerson was immensely impressed with her.

"I tell you, you're right, my young lady. However, these days I've a feeling New York is more like a stew of ideas and systems all competing for attention."

Emma smiled. All that was sweet and good in her heart and soul seemed to flow into her face that evening making her appear quite charming. She was star struck and had the time of her life. She talked to him about her poetry and he told her, among other things, "Each man has his own vocation, the talent is his call."

That night when Emma came home, she felt like dancing. She couldn't go to bed, so she stayed up writing. She took out her diary and wrote, "The Sage from Concord," a tall, spare figure crowned by a small head, beaked nose and piercing eyes, unforgettable eagle eyes, full of smiling wisdom. And guess what, he wants to read my poems. top that!"

## 8

# The Sage from Concord

Now that Mr. Emerson had said he was looking forward to reading Emma's poems, she couldn't be more delighted. Ralph Waldo Emerson was a good man and he particularly loved to encourage young, talented people like Henry David Thoreau and others. For a time, he financially supported Mr. Bronson Alcott, whose daughter, Louisa May, authored the all-time favorite book, *Little Women*. He paid Alcott's rent and helped him in many other ways.

But Emerson was known to be as a very demanding master as well. He expected tremendous effort so that one put out one's best work. Yet the gifted, for the most part, didn't mind that and actually found a great companion in him.

"Mr. Emerson is just like a father to me," Emma wrote in her journal. "He tells me to always do my best and be the best person I can be, just like Papa does. However, I find it far easier to do my best than always be on my best behavior. I don't quite know how to do that yet, but I promise to keep on trying."

Emma was set on becoming a poet and she had never changed her mind about that. She went to work, words streaming out of her like a river. She was a quick and spontaneous writer. The family's inside joke was that, "Emma could write fifteen thousand verses in two weeks."

Within a short time, she had a manuscript with new poems to send off to Emerson along with her book.

It turned out Mr. Emerson had been away from home traveling. Emma waited and waited, she eagerly looked for the morning mail, but a letter from Emerson was not anywhere in sight. The more she thought, the more she knew in her heart of hearts that she really wanted to be a poet more than anything in the whole wide world. However, as time went by, she started to despair. She even cried a little in secret.

Yet, no matter how bad Emma felt about herself, she always felt better after writing in her journal. "How stupid of me," she noted in her diary, "even to think that such a distinguished person was going to waste his precious time on me."

It was on February 24, 1868, when Emerson wrote his first letter to Emma. "I have happy recollections of the conversations we had at Mr. Ward's. I am so glad to have your book and letter which now more than confirm my first impressions." He'd read her poems and liked them, "The poems have important merits," he wrote.

Her poem "Brevet Brigadier: General Fred Winthrop" had a special effect on him. She had dedicated it to those who died in The Civil War and those who had survived it.

> "More hearts will break than gladden when
> The bitter struggle's past;
> The giant form of victory must
> A giant's shadow cast."

And another poem called forth by the war was "Heroes."

"Tender as flowers
Oh may, the thoughts
Of those
Who lie beneath the
Living beauty, dead...
Beneath the sunshine,
Blind."

That was the beginning of a correspondence between an unknown teenager and one of the most famous men of the time. To this nineteen-year-old girl, the letters from Concord became the highlight of her life. From then on, she began to look forward to the daily mail with eager anticipation.

# 9

# *A Slap in the Face*

*I*ndeed, Emerson kept his promise. In the spring of 1868, he was on a lecture tour to New York City and he put aside special time to spend with Emma, as he'd planned. Her emotions were over flowing; she could hardly contain herself. Her sisters waited eagerly for her to return home after that special meeting.

When Emma walked in, they all rushed to the foyer. There was excitement, laughter and a whole lot of commotion. Emma's face glowed. It was nearly too much for her to bear to be that happy.

The girls were especially curious. "So what did you talk about?" asked Josephine. Though she was happy for her, Emma could still detect a tinge of jealousy in her voice. After all, the man she went to see was the great sage that everybody so admired.

"Oh, it was great! My heart beat excitedly at first, but then I settled in. Mr. Emerson sort of made me feel at ease and I no longer had any reason to be nervous. He's so interesting to talk to, and so understanding."

"And ... and what did he say?" asked Sarah.

"He made some recommendations about how to improve my

37

writing even further. He said something to the effect that, 'Simple words and short sentences by far outweigh the more complicated forms of expression.' I'll have to keep that in mind, sometimes I get carried away and go on and on and on."

Annie laughed when she said, "on and on."

"That's all he said? What, then, took you so long?" asked Josephine.

"He also made suggestions about what I might like to read."

"Like what? I, myself, might want to read the books he suggested as well. It could be useful to learn words of wisdom ... perhaps..." said Josephine. "Well, here's two he mentioned: *Meditations* by Marcus Aurelius and also *Man's Origin and Destiny* by J.P. Lesley. And here's another he said I should read, and then sit for a while and write a poem." She pulled out a note pad, "Here it is, I've jotted it down: The *Bhagvat Gita*, in Charles Wilkin's translation. Mr. Emerson made a point that I get the best translation, otherwise I may not enjoy it quite as much."

Emma didn't share with her siblings, however, all of what she'd confided in her beloved mentor. "I've been having trouble lately with my moods," she said. "Sometimes I feel like I'm a seesaw. Full of love one minute, then the next, my spirit takes a dive."

Mr. Emerson understood the mood swings of the teenage years. "Oh, my dear girl, grief, passion and disaster are the materials of art."

Emma was relieved. He made it sound like it was fine, that everybody felt a little bit like that from time to time.

And after a short pause, Emerson went on to say, "An artist spends himself like the crayon in his hand, till he is all gone."

Her association with him became one of her most valued friendships. It fueled her creative fires and made her very productive.

When Emma's second book was published in 1869, the Lazarus sisters squeezed around Emma's desk with excited curiosity. Her voice was pitched slightly higher than usual when she said, "Guess who I dedicated the book to?"

They all opened their eyes wide and perked up their ears, but didn't make any guesses.

"To Emerson!" she said with great cheer, and then she went on to read it, "To my friend, Ralph Waldo Emerson."

She grinned from ear to ear.

Soon, however, the Lazarus family would have a heavy cloud hanging over their home. One day, out of the blue, their happy life was deeply marred by tragedy. They were shaken over the sudden death of Mrs. Lazarus' brother, Benjamin, son of Seixas Nathan, who'd been killed in a robbery in New York City.

A very strange and solemn feeling came over Emma as she stood there with no sound but the rustle of the trees outside. She saw the hurt on her mother's face when she heard the news. She frowned and suddenly looked very tired. Her gaze shifted from Mr. Lazarus to the children. Mr. Lazarus first looked sternly at the newspaper, then at the wall. Frank bit his lip to keep from crying. He had particularly liked Uncle Benjamin. Emma's head ached badly.

In the midst of such sad events, she wrote to Emerson to share the bad news with him. "My family is in shock, and my mother is especially heart-sore from losing her beloved brother. We grieved and attended the mourning service. Now, my dear mother is racked with coughs and aches. It's difficult to sooth her. I'm looking forward to seeing my Mom in high spirits once more."

Emma's friend in Concord responded right away and expressed his horror. Emerson mentioned that when he'd first read about the robbery in the papers, he'd glossed over it. "Without suspicion that it touched a friend of mine, my eyes rushed over the outrageous account."

Every single poem or play Emma wrote, she sent to Emerson. He wouldn't just merely praise her work, he would also comment with fine distinctions that showed his understanding of her gifts as well as her personality.

She wrote in her diary, "Mr. Emerson is a star that leads youthful hearts through periods of mental storm and struggle into safety. He is a lighthouse for those trying to find their way in life."

Josephine noticed how much he meant to Emma. She remarked,

"Sometimes, I think his books are bread and wine to you. When I watch you, I get the feeling that you absorb them into your very being."

Emma was a little bit shy about how important Emerson was to her. She tilted her head to the side and smiled. It was true, she enjoyed her friendship with Emerson, and his letters were full of appreciation and warm regard. That in it self was an incentive that lifted her spirit and encouraged her to put forth her best efforts. Besides, he was charming and popular; and possessed the ability to light up her mind and to stimulate her creative life.

A few years later, though, something happened she would have thought impossible. Over breakfast one morning, Mr. Lazarus turned to Emma and asked, "And how is my genius doing?"

"Guess what, Papa, Mr. Emerson prepared a huge anthology of English poetry."

"Is that so? How large is it?" asked Josephine.

"I believe it must be almost a thousand columns. English and American poems printed side by side for the first time. Isn't that a wonderful idea?"

"Sounds interesting," said Mr. Lazarus.

"That is interesting," added Mrs. Lazarus "American poetry is every bit as good as is that of the English poets."

"What's it called?" Josephine asked.

"Ah, he calls it *Parnassus*. I can hardly wait to see it. It just makes me wonder which one of my poems he has picked."

When the book finally arrived, she quickly leafed through it and saw names like Howard Barnes, H.H, and contemporaries from Boston, New York and Philadelphia. Seeing their work she knew that she would most certainly find her name as well because their work seemed not to have greater merit than hers. Emma, however, had trouble finding her name. She turned to the Table of Contents. Her eyes ran down the alphabet and stopped at the letter L. She backed up to check under E. She was not on the list. Was that possible? "I can't believe this," she said to herself. "How could that be? He who had praised and loved her poems had now turned and rejected them?"

# 10

## *She Failed*

*N*othing seemed to make sense to Emma. Suddenly she had a feeling this was all a show, everything was a pretense, no one was ever, ever going to tell her the truth again. Everything seemed very strange as they all sat around the fireplace, Mr. Lazarus in the big chair with Frank at his feet and Sarah and Josephine perched on either arm of the chair. Emma was leaning on the back of the chair so no one could see any sign of her sad feelings should someone bring up the topic of how Emerson had left her out of his book of poetry. She felt tired, thoughts dotted her mind like a swirl of flies, some circling out, some coming in.

Mrs. Lazarus entered the room and broke the silence by saying to Emma, "I watched your efforts to control yourself." She patted Emma on the head and kissed her on the cheek. A huge tear dropped off the end of Emma's nose as she hid her face in her mother's shoulder and began to sob.

"Moses, I'm telling you," said Esther. "Oh dear, a poet's life is very trying."

He only nodded.

Seeing Emma saddened by tears, the sisters wanted to comfort her, but they had nothing really helpful to offer. They were also surprised.

Annie ran over to her and laid her head on Emma's arm.

The girls wore sad, troubled expressions as if they, too, experienced her disappointment. Nobody talked much. They seemed to be sitting and waiting for the coffee pot to boil. The fragrance coming from the kitchen was inviting.

Now Emma felt her heart was broken, "It is as if there was an earthquake," she said with a whisper of a voice, wiping off her tears.

Sarah didn't seem to know what to say. She could only point to a box of chocolate mints that lay on the table. It helped to change the mood a bit, even though it was a small thing.

"Have you seen Felix Effrey's chocolate store?" asked Josephine. "It's right around the corner at Broadway and 9th Street."

Frank licked his lips and said, "I love to watch their window and see the wheel go round." His hands swirled in circles.

"Now they have three white stone rollers," said Moses, "and they grind the chocolate into paste all day long."

Emma felt a sneeze starting in her nose. The sneeze erupted from her, and again, and again, and again. "My ear is clogged," she said in frustration.

Frank chimed in, "I've got a new joke. It's a good one, too. Listen to this. Tom walks into a hardware store, and asks the storekeeper, 'Do you have any rat poison?' The man says, 'Yes. Do you want to get some?' To which Tom says, 'Oh, no. I'll just get my rats over to you.'"

Frank Eliezer grinned while the others chuckled. Emma was self-absorbed. There was no telling whether she was even listening.

Josephine mentioned how she'd spent hours at A.T. Stewart's, the famous department store. It was known as Stewart's "marble palace" because it was a six-story marble building that stretched over a block on the east side of Broadway between Chambers and Reade Street.

"I wanted to get me a new hat, the kind with the flowers," said Josephine, "but I couldn't make up my mind. They've got too many to choose from."

"Hey, what do you think of their new displays? Aren't they great?" said Mary. "Especially the silks and the gloves. Emma, you must see them. These dresses from Paris are stunning, especially the French laces."

Emma just listened but made no comment. For a little while, her sisters squabbled over who should wear what kind of hat and whose face is round or oval shaped.

"Actually," said Mrs. Lazarus to change the subject, "I ought to see if they've got the Irish linen that I've been waiting for."

"Oh, you may want to see the paisley and cashmere shawls as well," said Josephine as she touched her neck. "They are just gorgeous."

"Emma," her mother tried to draw her into the conversation, "why don't you come with me?"

Emma just shook her head.

"But, you'll have to help me stay away from John Taylor's ice cream saloon," she continued with a smile.

"Oh, you mean the one on Broadway and Franklin Street," confirmed Sarah. "It's gotten so fashionable lately, don't you think?"

"Why of course," said Mr. Lazarus, "that's the only place in town where ladies are being served even when they come without a male companion, unlike other places."

"The only problem I've got with their ice cream," Mrs. Lazarus chuckled, putting her hands on her hips, "is it causes my constricted waistline to bend out of shape!"

The girls smiled. Even Emma's lips moved up a tiny bit at the corners.

Frank got up and brought over the box of chocolates, popped one into his mouth and puffed himself up as he was in the habit of doing when he was getting ready for mischief of one kind or another.

"He likes to poke fun at women's gestures," Emma thought.

"See, on windy days ..." said Frank mimicking a woman trying to hold onto her hat with one hand while grasping the shopping bag with the other. He pretended to walk with difficulty, in the manner of women who wore very tight clothing.

Emma watched silently as he was horsing around. He bumped into the leg of a chair and pressed his shoes hard against the carpet. He bent his knees, and as he tried to catch his balance, his right foot caught the corner of the rug and he tumbled down. He almost rolled into Annie's lap.

"Frank!" Mrs. Lazarus called out sternly.

"Sorry," Frank apologized.

Annie made some funny faces and gave a few squeaky sounds to call attention to herself. The girls couldn't help laughing and felt better for it. The sight of Frank carrying on made Emma sober again.

Mr. Lazarus got out of his chair, straightened himself up and looked around.

Emma wanted to go to her Papa, but she averted his eyes. Maybe she was embarrassed for him to see her being a "failure."

Her father put on his glasses, saying slowly, "I suggest you turn over a new leaf and begin again."

Emma gazed at her shoes to avoid his eyes.

"My dear girl, listen to me, there's nothing like good, hard work to get you going again." He looked so strong and sensible and kind as he put his hand on her shoulder, flicked his eyebrows and smiled.

Emma's eyes kept filling with tears in spite of herself.

"It's all right," her father said and gave her a hug. He was getting ready to leave the house.

Emma went into her room feeling a little faint; she looked sorrowfully out the window. It was so full of light and bustle outside, yet so gloomy and still inside Emma's room. "All these worries and disappointments," she thought, "are like little mosquitoes. I must be sensible again."

Out of the blue, she suddenly recalled a few lines from a popular Ragtime song, "clouds will soon roll, you can fly, if you try, if you try..."

## 11

## *But Why?*

*E*mma lay back in her chair toying with her hair while looking out the window through half-closed lids. It seemed no one could redeem the situation. "And I believed every word he had written," she thought. "What a fool I was."

She sat with her head in her hands for a long time.

The room was now totally silent. It seemed as if time was standing still. Emma began to look back into the past recalling the dinner party where she had first met Emerson. He had been so kind and charming and sincere.

What greater assurance could she have of great hopes for the future? "How impressed he was with me and my writing," she thought. "There was something so wise about him." She replayed these thoughts over and over again.

"I'll never be the kind of poet I long to be in my inner most heart. How could I? I have no talent. I was misled by what I wished to believe. Now, I'd better forget the hopes and dreams I was born with and face reality."

Perhaps she would never write again, she thought. From now on, her days would have an entirely different pattern. She would have the kind of life other young women had: shopping, arranging dinner parties and meeting with friends for lunch. These thoughts only made her feel more tired.

Emma willed herself to get up from her chair. Although her steps were light and silent, it seemed to her that she was trudging across the room to get to her bed. Weary from the long day, she finally fell asleep.

The next morning she was awakened earlier than usual by the hard, white and uneasy light pouring into her room. She took the weather as an omen, her abrupt awakening as a sign, and thought of what she wanted to say to Emerson. She dressed carefully. When she looked at herself in the mirror, she thought she looked presentable.

Emma went to the kitchen, poured herself a cup of coffee and took it back into her room. From her window, she saw the wind blowing and a little branch kept swinging backwards and forwards. The sun disappeared and suddenly it seemed cloudy, but there were no distinct clouds, just shades of gray all over the sky.

Finally, she moved over to the little table, took a sheet of paper and wrote, "36 West 14 St., December 27th 1874. My dear Mr. Emerson." Now, in a strange way, in the silent and dim room, Emma felt her own disappointment and sadness dissolve. The anger that was underneath began to stir, to increase, to take over. The two lines between her eyebrows deepened. And at this very early hour, she felt her heart beat. Emma tightened her lips. She demanded Emerson explain why her name was missing from his selections.

She wrote him a strong letter saying, "I cannot resist ... expressing to you my extreme disappointment. Your favorable opinion having been confirmed by some of the best critics in England and America."

Emma, once launched, was not to be sidetracked. She went on to say, "I felt as if I had won for myself, by my own efforts, a place for myself in any collection of American poetry and I find myself treated with absolute contempt in the very quarter where I had been encouraged to build my fondest hopes."

What she meant was that she was being treated unfairly because Emerson, who had encouraged her all along, now turned around and rejected her. Writing was much too important for Emma to just ignore the hurt.

Her writing table was decked with flowers. She wore a rather beautiful blue lapis pendant that matched the deep blue lilacs that sat before her. She reread her letter, put it in an envelope and sealed it. A calmness came over Emma; the storm had passed. A heavy stone was lifted off her heart. She picked up her letter and walked with determination out of the room.

# 12

## When Sorrow Comes

*E*arly in 1876, Emma's mother died. It was a drizzly morning. The sight of men and women huddled against the wind who had come to bury her mother made Emma's heart feel many shades of grieving and mourning.

As they chanted the Aramaic words "Yit'gadal v'yit'kadash Shmey rabbah ...(Magnified and sanctified may His great Name be)..." Emma thought, "We're burying the one we love," and she felt dreary deep inside her heart.

The rabbi later instructed Mr. Lazarus to read Psalm 23, "The Lord is my shepherd; I shall not want. He maketh me to lie down in green pastures. He leadeth me beside the still waters. He restoreth my soul..."

Emma and her siblings stepped closer to the grave. A pain shot through her body each time the mourning Kaddish was recited. Warm memories and love came and went. She recalled when her mother had said, "I want my children to be good, loved, respected, accomplished and wise." How her face was full of soft loveliness and her voice had tenderness in it.

Following the funeral, the family spent seven days of Shivah at home during which they could mourn and express their grief among family and friends. Many came to pay Shivah calls. Among them was Jacob Hart Lazarus, Emma's Uncle. He was one of New York's most accomplished portrait artists. On her mother's side, she had seventy first cousins, all prominent in the social, political and literary life of the city. Now, many of them were reminiscing and sharing comforting memories.

"One winter, Mom and Dad," Emma recalled, "had hired a stage sleigh to take all of us for a ride down Broadway to the Battery and back."

"I remember," said Josephine. "The sleigh was open and very, very long."

"And it had long seats on each side," said Emma.

"I especially liked the straw on the floor; it kept my feet warm."

"The sleigh bells were my favorite things," Frank added. "They filled the air with cheerful sounds, it was great fun."

Then, one of the cousins mentioned how Washington Square and Union Square, right around the corner from the Lazarus', had been places where Elizabeth Cady Stanton, along with other women, had demonstrated and demanded voting rights along with personal, social and political freedom.

"But on quiet days," said Emma "my friend and I used to roll our hoops and jump rope in one of these Squares."

"And I liked the fun we had on the merry-go-round on Lafayette Place," said Frank. "It used to be at the Vauxhall Gardens."

When the visitors left, Emma sat for a while looking at her father and wondering, "Why did mother have to die? What happens when you die? I want to know more about dying things."

Annie's voice broke the silence, "I don't want to die. I'm sort of scared."

Moses wrapped his arms around his little girl in a heartfelt embrace. Slightly choked up, he said, "You've got nothing to worry about, Annie. You've a whole life ahead of you."

"But why do people die?" Annie insisted.

"Dying," said Moses, "is a stage in life that nobody understands, a great mystery for all of us."

Emma sat thinking about how her mother had grown old, tired and had a thin white face. Then doctors had announced there was no hope.

Josephine stood with her hands crossed over her chest, looking perplexed. Agnes sat on one arm of the chair.

Emma felt restless in the face of this solemn situation. She got up, parted the curtains and stood between them and the window. Her mind was in turmoil. She'd suddenly realized that people didn't give much thought to what really mattered in life.

Now, she didn't know whether the world was an amazing dream or more like a giant jigsaw puzzle. She wished she had some kind of explanation of how everything fit together because she felt she knew almost nothing about life.

Emma asked herself, "What is my mission here on earth?" Brimming with all sorts of questions made her feel even lonelier and much sadder.

That evening, Mr. Lazarus was also lost in his thoughts and feelings and didn't say a whole lot.

The only thing that lit up the darkness, Emma felt inside, was the full moon outside.

As the days went by, she noticed her father stopped going to his favorite clubs. He'd been a member of the exclusive Union Club, and he was one of the founders of the Knickerbockers Club along with William Astor, William Vanderbilt and others. She knew he had enjoyed spending time in these places. There he saw friends, wrote letters and dined from time to time.

The Lazarus' were a close-knit family. Now that the children had lost their beloved mother, Moses wanted to be there for them, and they needed him more than ever before.

## 13

## *Emma in Concord*

*E*mma, Emma, you've got a letter," Annie hollered as she ran into her sister's room.

It wasn't just any letter, it was a letter from Emerson. She jumped up from her chair; she couldn't believe it was true. After a year and a half of complete silence, Emerson surprised her. Not only that, he had invited her to spend a week with his family in Concord. Emma was thrilled. "There isn't anything more in the world I'd have wished for than that," she thought. Besides, she hoped to find out why she had not been included in his poetry collection.

It was perfect, just what she needed. Since she'd lost her mother, she'd hoped a short trip to her favorite mentor would be a change of pace that could help her heal.

She looked forward to the adventure of traveling alone. At the time, Emma was 27, and that would be the first time in her life she would travel by herself. That was very unusual in those days; most girls traveled with their families and friends.

In August 1876, Emma took the train to Concord.

As the train zoomed by one slope of hills that was green, while another was already in bright colors, she marveled at the shimmering display of colors. In the strong sunshine, the leaves appeared bright and clear. The Ginkgo trees sizzled with glowing yellows. Emma was delighted when she arrived in Concord at last.

"Pleased to see you," she was greeted by Emerson's lit-up face and his warm smile. He came with his little one-horse wagon to meet her at the train station. Emma noticed how distinguished looking he was at seventy-three with his white hair.

As he drove her to his home, she couldn't take her eyes off his long, quiet and pleasant face. "He's giving up all this time from his writing just for me," she thought secretly, and her eyes lightened while her heart bounced with joy.

His house was gray and square with dark green window shades set among trees and a little garden. As they walked in, he introduced her to his second wife, Lidian, and his thirty-seven year old daughter, Ellen, a Sunday schoolteacher.

"From your letter," she said to Ellen, "I gathered you were a serious kind of person."

Ellen laughed.

"Are you equally surprised about me?" asked Emma.

"I think not," said Ellen. "You are what I already knew you must be."

Emma saw a painting in the hallway. It was an erupting volcano. "Ah," she thought, "he so often uses this image to describe the deep feelings poets try to express." On one of his many bookshelves, she noticed the great German author Goethe's works. A line that particularly caught her attention said, "He who cannot draw on three-thousand years is living from hand to mouth."

"Hum, that's interesting; I wonder what he meant by that," Emma thought.

From the steeple, a bell tolled the hour. After dinner, as Emma looked out, night was gathering in the quiet streets. Darkness veiled the mountains. Ellen told her that usually at 8:00 p.m., they call it a night.

But when the time came, Emma asked, "Is Mr. Emerson going to bed, too? If he is going to sit up, may I sit up, too?"

Ellen and her mother consented. So, Emma spent the next half-hour in his company, and at 8:30 p.m., she went up to her room.

Emma looked in the mirror and saw a careful, distinguished young woman. As she combed back her shiny hair, she marveled at the design of the dresser and passed her hand lightly over one of its doors. She knew once she was at home and lying in bed, she would not remember that piece of furniture, but would always remember the drive with Emerson from the train station.

She sat for a while on the edge of her bed to take in the peace of the room. She listened for him and wondered how he spent his days.

In the morning, Emma waited at the front door to meet him. At 10:30 a.m., she turned to Nina, the housekeeper, and asked, "Where is Mr. Emerson?"

"Oh, he is always shut up in the study until dinner time."

Emma knew he was a busy man; he had to read and prepare for his speaking engagements. "His ability with words is so marvelous," she mused. "How he strikes at people's hearts, often with one sentence only. Like the time when he said, 'The reward of a thing well done is having done it.' I love that." She took out a book she had brought along. Emma began thinking, "He always encourages me to trust my own thought."

It was quite amusing what he had said last night. "In this world," he said, "if a man sits down to think, he is immediately asked if he has a headache." She sensed the smile in her eyes and the corners of her mouth as they turned up.

At 11:00 a.m., Ellen took Emma for a ride to the cliffs. She was taken by the splendid view. She told Ellen, "Living in New York and Newport, I'm not used to such spacious landscape."

Emma enjoyed the little streams, how they overlapped and interlaced with one another. She later wrote in her diary that Concord seemed to her, "Lovely and smiling with its quiet meadows, quiet slopes and quietest of rivers."

She also loved the crunch and crackle of the leaves under foot. They passed children playing in piles of leaves, throwing them into the air like confetti and leaping into the soft orange and gold beds they made. "How many people live in Concord?" asked Emma.

"Oh, we have 2,021 people here. This town is considered a healthy place."

"You mean by being close to nature?" said Emma.

"Yes. Many people here live to be seventy and over compared with other places where the average is only forty-eight."

"Besides," Emma added, "Boston is nearby. That makes it really special."

Ellen told Emma about her Great Aunt Mary Moody Emerson and how she used to come and visit the family when her father was still a boy. She had taken him for nature walks and always had some interesting things to discuss with him. "She was a transcendentalist who believed that people could have a more personal experience with the Divine, an experience, she believed, that it is available to every person. In fact, she started the movement." Emma now knew who had influenced Emerson to become a transcendentalist. She also had an opportunity to meet some of the New England writers and thinkers she admired so much who were also transcendentalist.

All and all, she'd spent an exciting week in Concord with Emerson. She visited Brownson Alcott, the critic. He was a witty man but, "I don't care much for his opinions," she thought. She also met Emerson's disciple, Franklin Benjamin Sanborn, and his wife.

Later she described in her diary the afternoon she'd spent with William Ellery Channing, the poet and biographer of Thoreau. She wrote, "I sat with him in the sunlit woods looking at the gorgeous blue and silver summer sky. He guided me through the woods and pointed out the site of Thoreau's famous hut. A few steps beyond the pond with thickly wooded shores, everything exquisitely peaceful and beautiful in the afternoon light, and not a sound would be heard except the crickets or the 'z-ing' of locusts which Thoreau described." She titled these entries, "Persons that Pass and Shadows that Remain."

Before leaving Concord, Channing gave her two parting gifts. One was his own book on Thoreau and the other was Thoreau's pocket compass. The gifts touched her heart and she held back tears of gratitude as they shook hands farewell.

When it was time to say good-by, Emerson gave her the proof sheets of the five-act play *Spagnoletto* she'd written. He said he liked it. "He is so fatherly to me," she mused. "Something in him flows out to people like a flood of light, what a gentle and kind man."

The visit with Emerson was all Emma had hoped it would be. Though she wanted to ask him why she had not been included in his anthology, she didn't, nor did he mention it.

# 14

## On the Move

On the way back from Concord, sometimes the sun burned through, sometimes it stayed behind the clouds. It was just as hot either way. Her siblings could hardly wait to see her. "I missed you," said Annie.

Sarah said, "We all missed you."

"Oh, and I missed you," said Emma.

"Wait until you see the pile of letters you've got waiting for you," Josephine said, preparing her.

"From whom?"

"You're not going to believe it."

Emma was thrilled to learn she had letters from famous writers and thinkers like Robert Browning, William James, James Russell Lowell and Ivan Turgenev.

"Look at this one, it's from the *North American Review*. They've published my article." Her spirit soared in delight. "Papa, you're not going to believe this. My name is in the same magazine with Emerson!"

"That's my girl."

"Now I can brag about my famous sister," Frank Eliezer chimed in.

Emma smiled and gave him a hug. "My silly brother," she felt fresh beginnings in the air. Moses Lazarus bought a new house further uptown at 34 East 57th Street. Everyone was busy taking down items and packing them into cartons and boxes of various sizes.

"Things are falling apart down here," said Frank.

Emma looked up and saw her father removing the brocade curtains with the green silk under-curtains that were across the room. "The place is a mess," she said. As she searched for more cartons in one of the closets, she stopped in front of the three beautiful portraits that hung on the walls admiring the dignity of three generations on her mother's side. She heard Josephine's voice; it sounded urgent and excited.

"What is it?" Emma called back.

Josephine pointed to the middle of the dining room. She was the one with a checklist to make sure nothing would be forgotten. Emma took it to mean that the wall hangings had to come down. I always loved these foliage tapestries, she reminisced; they had the richness and softness of velvet.

Then suddenly, she cried out in excitement, "Hey, I've uncovered a treasure, stacks and stacks of plates. These must be mother's wedding dishes. I never knew she had so much stuff."

Emma sorted out shoes and dresses. Some she had outgrown and she discarded, others she gave away.

Each item was a memory. Emma wrapped up large hats, sweaters, knives, forks, spoons, a bottle opener and combs. Her older sisters were helping with the books; there were shelves and shelves of them. Porters and movers rumbled, pushed and pulled as they lifted cartons and furniture.

On the eve of the move, Emma sat in her room for the last time. "It is with deepest regret that I'm leaving this place," she pondered. But the house had recently witnessed her mother's death which made it heavy with the sadness of her memory. She took Emerson's photograph off her mantelpiece and put it in her book of poems.

After settling into the new house, Emma was eager to get back to writing. One day, as she leafed through her periodicals, she called out, "Look! Look!"

Her sisters came immediately and all at once cried out, "Oh!"

Moses got up from the sofa, "What's all this excitement?" he asked.

"Guess," said Frank.

"I've got an entire front page in *Henry Ward Beecher's Non-Denominational Weekly!*"

Moses nodded, "That's a prestigious paper." He took the paper from Emma and read out loud the titles of her two poems, "Loving Mother" and "Sympathy." Emma felt her cheeks glow with pleasure.

"Why don't you ever write about men and baldness for a change?" Frank chuckled and everyone else smiled.

These poems were about mothers from all over the world, sharing in good moments and in times of sorrow, in joy and in tears while caring for their children.

Some days, Emma would recline in her chair reading her manuscripts carefully through looking for periods and dashes here and there or spotting other punctuation needing her attention. As her interests spread in range, she began to express herself in new ways in her writing.

"I like variety," she mused. "And I enjoy trying my hand in fresh forms." On occasion, she would write short plays or articles on important artists. At other times, she would write critical essays or book reviews.

In the late 1870s, the name Emma Lazarus became well-known to American writers. They were introduced to her writings through such publications as *Lippincott's, Century, The Atlantic Monthly*, and the *American Hebrew.*

"You aren't going to guess what I read today," said Sarah.

Emma looked at her with eyes wide open.

"They say you're the best female conversationalist of our time. 'She is witty and sharp,' their exact words. When I mentioned it to Aunt Amelia, she laughed and said,..."

Emma was amused by that and finished the sentence, "Emma's always on fire about something!"

"Precisely."

Her writing continued to soar. The poem "The Taming of a Falcon" was published in the *Century's* special issue of the decade. It was featured under "Poems of American Women."

Yet, she was not satisfied with this new recognition. She expected much more of herself and wanted to make a difference in the world. She longed to feel that her life really mattered.

Emma confided in her friend Edmund Clarence Stedman, a famous editor, who lived nearby. "I have accomplished nothing to stir, nothing to awaken, to teach or to suggest, nothing that the world could not equally well do without."

To this he replied, "Have you never thought of your own heritage?"

The two frequently discussed and argued about writers and ideas. However, this time she was puzzled.

"I mean your Jewish heritage. There's a wealth of tradition you are heir to and you could use as a source of inspiration."

Emma stood silent for a second. Then she looked up a bit to the left trying to remember. "What about that long, ambitious piece I've written based on Jewish history: "The Dance of Death." It was about Jews in Germany in the Middle Ages. They were accused of causing the Black Plague." But that was the work Emma had put into a desk drawer and shown to no one.

"I've written about Jews of the past and their poets," she thought, "but I don't believe that a writer can be truly important who is not involved in what's happening in the world."

Emma wanted to be inspired by the life around her. Yet, she did not have that strong an interest in the Jews in New York City. How could she be their poet? Now that Clarence Stedman had mentioned the idea of writing about her heritage, she recalled she had written a few poems that had a Jewish background. Not only that, but Dr. Gustav Gotheil, rabbi of Temple Emanuel of New York, had asked her to translate several Jewish hymns from the German as well.

"After I'd done that," she recalled, "he further encouraged me to compose some original hymns of my own for his new hymnal. But I had to decline. I told him I've no feeling for religion. Yet, I am very proud of my Jewish culture and my Jewish ancestors."

Struggling to find direction, she turned to another Jewish poet, Heinrich Heine. He was also concerned with his Jewishness and claimed he liked only the Jewish writings but not the religious lifestyle. She threw herself into his German poetry and discovered a brilliant poet. (Unfortunately, his career had been cut short by his early death.)

"I'm fascinated by his 'not–Jewish' Jewishness. I can identify with him," she thought. On other occasions, she shared with her siblings that she'd felt he mirrored the life she was living. "In an odd sort of way," she said, "he helps me to understand myself somewhat better."

"But he converted to Christianity," said Agnes.

"You know why?" Emma leaped to his defense.

"No. Why?"

"He'd hoped to find employment. He was a lawyer, but German regulations had discriminated against Jews, and he could not practice law. However, his conversion hadn't helped him either. Disappointed, he picked himself up and went to Paris."

With great enthusiasm, Emma set out to work. She translated many of his poems, put them in a book and introduced them along with Heine's biography. Her translations of *Poems and Ballads by Heinrich Heine* were highly praised by *The New York Times*.

Stedman, her editor friend, told Emma, "I stayed up past midnight reading these poems. They are very subtle and very spirited."

She was really pleased. Her hard work had paid off. But now she needed a vacation. In 1879, she visited Emerson for a second time. She told her friend Helena about her visit. "I found Mr. Emerson very sadly changed and much older than when I saw him last but with the same wonderful benign dignity of expression and bearing, and the same sincere wisdom of thought as before."

This time he shared a funny story with her about his Aunt Mary Moody Emerson. One day when Thoreau's mother visited her wearing pink ribbons, his aunt shut her eyes and talked with her for a while.

After some time, Mary Emerson said, "Mrs. Thoreau, I don't know whether or not you observed that my eyes are shut."

"Yes, Madam, I have observed it."

"Perhaps, you would like to know the reason?"

"Yes, I would."

"I don't like to see a person of your age guilty of such levity in her dress."

Emerson said his aunt could get away with saying that because she had an outspoken character. Emma smiled.

# 15

## *Chocolate Sauce City*

"*N*ow, don't laugh," wrote Emma to her friend, Helena deKay Gilder. "I lost my head musically. Berlioz' Faust has made a great sensation in New York and I have heard it six times during the last ten days, each time with interested delight. I am eagerly looking forward to one final hearing of it tomorrow evening. The last time I heard it, it was with your brother."

Emma was good friends with Helena and her husband, Richard. Whenever she had anything intimate, emotional gossipy or thoughtful on her mind, she would confide in her. The Gilder's home became the gathering place for the best and the brightest actors, artists, musicians and public figures. She was not only friends with the Gilders but also with their families, especially with Helena's brother, Charlie. Furthermore, it was rumored Charles deKay and Emma were in love. He escorted her to concerts, the theatre and many other cultural events. One evening, as they were walking, happy and light hearted, she commented, "I'm beginning to see that John La Farge was right."

"John is a painter with revolutionary ideas," Charlie agreed.

"No question. You know what he said at our meeting last week?"

"No. What?"

"That these brownstones are everywhere and that the city needs a new face. Come to think of it, when you see one, you have seen them all."

"Our town is covered with a cold chocolate sauce, don't you think?" She laughed and looked up into his smiling eyes.

Day and night one could see workers in the streets, above the streets and under the streets. The rattle and rumble of cranes and drills were background music everywhere. The only thing steady in New York was continuous change. It was built, then demolished, to be built again, in another way, for another purpose.

During a slight lull in the conversation, Emma said, "It really is 'the city that's never finished.'"

Charlie gave a sigh of admiration.

Both of them ambled across to the seaport, enjoying the magnificent view of ships coming in and going out. Just above them, cranes swung, horns sounded and workers shouted. Startled by the whistle of a steamer, Emma looked up. It was a moonlight night and so beautiful she thought she was dreaming.

Charlie commented, "Edison really dressed this city up with these flickering electric streetlights."

"It's breathtaking. I encourage all my friends to come into Manhattan just for the lights, it is a real treat."

"See, over here is the link to the news from Europe and the new ideas newcomers bring over," said Charles.

Emma gazed at him and their eyes met, "Now I feel that you, *The New York Times* editor, are giving me a guided tour."

He laughed. She saw happiness reflected in his face and liked that.

"You've made quite a reputation for yourself."

"But not as a poet," he said.

"I love your poems." She liked them even though she knew most people didn't care for them and thought they were a bit strange.

"If you notice," Charles was talking about the city again, "the harbor makes it easy and very convenient to ship out cartons of books and all other printed matter to countries around the world."

"And that, in turn," she quickly figured out, "makes the most important publishers want to be in New York."

"Exactly, in fact, that's why New York's become such a remarkable, creative center affecting the culture all over America."

She thought of the bigness and wonder of destiny. Meeting Charlie had been a surprise and so was the future, and they would be together if life saw fit.

"Yes, I know," she said. "Anyone who wants a career in literature and journalism is dreaming of New York. Even in the small towns, everybody seems to know about the 'literary life' of our town of towns."

"Not anywhere else, only here," he lifted up his hand.

After dining at Purell's restaurant, Emma said, "Think we should go back?"

"I suppose so," Charles agreed reluctantly. With clasped hands and lighted eyes, they parted for the night.

She couldn't sleep. "He's a good man," she thought. "He has tender manners and he's cute. We always have lots to talk about. I think I love him. We are close but not close; something divides us. I'm not clear what that might be."

She recalled the burning blush that crept all over her when Charlie had said, "The voice of your eyes is deeper than words."

Come to think of it, there was something else he mentioned. Ah, I know, he pointed out that I was different than other young Jewish women. "In what way?" she had asked.

"They are forward, pert and bad mannered," he said.

She knew her Hebrew friends would agree with him. "If the truth be told, some of the Jews from the lower classes seem kind of rude to me as well," she admitted to herself.

Her thoughts kept her awake. Since she couldn't make herself fall asleep, she figured she might as well stay up and read. Rabbi Gottheil had lent her a book of legends of the Talmud, *Genesis Rabbah*. As she leafed through it, the story of the creation of man caught her eye. It was about the commotion in heaven before man came into being. While some angels were all for it, others thought it was not a good idea to create man.

That legend lit up Emma's imagination. She brushed the hair out of her eyes and words came flowing from her heart into her pen. She titled that poem "The Birth of Man."

"Lo, the divine idea of making man
Had spread abroad among the heavenly hosts;
With wind opposed, and contradicting cries:
'Fulfill, great Father, thine exalted thought!
Cease, cease, Almighty God! Create no more!'

And suddenly ... the angel Mercy knelt,
and thus he spoke,
'Fulfill, great Father, thine exalted thought!
Create the likeness of thyself on earth.
In this new creature, I will breathe the spirit
Of a divine compassion; he shall be
Thy fairest image in the universe.'

But to his words the angel Peace replied,
With heavy sobs: '...,
But man, the strange new being, everywhere
Shall bring confusion, trouble discord, war.'

A cloud of grief, and stillness deep prevailed.
Then from the midst of that abyss of light
..., these words rang forth: '... Truth I send
To be companion unto man on 'earth.'

'From heaven to earth, from earth once more to heaven,
Shall Truth with constant interchange, alight
And soar again, an everlasting link
Between the world and the sky.'

And man was born."

Emma played with a lock of her hair as she reread her verses. "We humans, on our own, would not know how to live," she mused. "Wisdom has to be supplied. We need to know how to act responsibly." She scratched her forehead. "That's why our people needed the Ten Commandments so we can be free to choose to be kind or to be mean. Desire, fear, greed and pride can, and do, warp human choices. I believe our job, of course, is to continue the creation of ourselves and to choose goodness and growth."

She got up, looked in the mirror and saw her face had a new light. Suddenly, she was filled with love for people and was moving about the room as if newly energized. She walked over to the window and stood there for some time.

"Come to think of it," she mused, "I remember a famous legend I once read that was about the Maharal, a rabbi who'd lived in Prague in the sixteen century. That holy man was empowered to create a golem out of clay, inscribe his forehead with the sacred name of God and send that living effigy to save the Jews when they suffered persecution."

"I guess that could be an idea to write." She tossed it over in her mind. "I could write about someone more familiar, though. Many have heard of Rashi, his explanations are practically on every page of the Bible. He was a holy man as well." She rubbed her eyes, "Now, though, I need to get some sleep," Emma reminded herself.

Pictures and thoughts rushed in and out of her head. "Emerson, my dear Emerson, I hear he's doing better," she recalled Ellen telling her. She'd given a ball in Concord's Town Hall to celebrate her birthday. She had invited two or three hundred of her friends and acquaintances. Emma pictured them dancing to the sounds of music. She thought the party must have created great excitement for that quaint little village.

In her mind's eye, she saw herself and Charlie at the concert again, and she smiled.

# 16

## Red Skies

The summer of 1880 passed very quickly. Emma and Charlie continued spending time together and going to concerts. On occasion, Helena, Charlie's sister and Emma's close friend, would join them with her husband, Richard.

One night, Mr. Lazarus came hurrying into the dining room. Emma was helping to set up the table.

"I have just heard terrible news," Moses said as he sat down.

"About?" Frank asked.

"Here, take a look at this," he pulled out *The New York Times* and pointed to the headlines on the front page.

"Attacks on Jews in Russia," he continued reading. "Suddenly, without any warning Jews are being attacked by raids of Russian soldiers returning from the Czar's war. Many Jews are now victims of organized massacres. These acts of violence are called pogroms."

He gave the paper to Emma, "Here, you read it to us. I think you ought to know what's going on over there."

She folded the paper and began reading about the soldiers who roamed the countryside robbing farms and setting them on fire. It told how Jews were beaten and murdered. Men, women and children ran in all direction only to find that all ways of escape were blocked off.

The article went on to describe how some pressed as close as they could against the wall of a building to melt into it, hoping they wouldn't be discovered. The attackers pulled the beards of elder rabbis and religious leaders. Many were flung down and beaten until bleeding.

"I just can't understand," Emma said. "They can't do that!"

Her father was at a loss for words, only his eyes spoke, they expressed sadness, pain and worry.

"But how dare they do that?" Emma insisted.

Mr. Lazarus sighed.

She noticed another headline telling of a mass meeting in London to protest these pogroms.

In New York, the former Secretary of State, William Evarts, spoke out. Emma had met him on several social occasions. This time she came to the rally because he'd personally asked her to attend.

When she returned home that night, one thing he'd said stuck in her mind, "The death of innocent men and women." These words wouldn't let go of her, they pinched her heart and filled her with a sense of urgency. She was very troubled. "I must do something," she said to herself.

As fate would have it, in April that year, the same issue of *Century* magazine carried an article Emma had written and another one that was written by a woman historian. Her name was Madame Ragozin, and her article was titled: "Russian Jews and Gentiles: From a Russian Point of View."

In it, she blamed the Jews for the pogroms, saying, "Where there is smoke there is fire." In other words, she believed that Jews must have done something to deserve the violence. "They are more concerned with saving their money than their manly honor," she wrote. "That's why Jews always retreated," according to her.

After reading that article, Emma was outraged. Right away she went to see the editor, R.W. Gilder, and convinced him an attack like that required a swift response in the very next issue of the *Century*.

"I'm ready to take on the defense of the Jews," she said, "if no one else is available for the task."

Emma worked hard on the research and soon finished her reply to the Russian woman's attacks. "The thirst of the Jew is not for money," she wrote, "but for knowledge. In those districts of Poland and Russia where they are not admitted to the schools, they have had books of natural science translated into Hebrew in order to be informed with the new ideas of the time..."

Oh, how to raise the spirit of Russian Jews, that became her mission. She wanted them to believe a brighter future was possible if everybody pulled together. She remembered the words of Thomas Carlyle, a famous writer at the time, "Tell a man he is brave, and you help him to become so."

Emma figured the opposite must be equally true. When people like Madame Rogozin accuse Jews by saying they are to blame for being helpless, Jews are led to be helpless. "I've an idea," she thought. "Jews had a heroic past!"

She took out her diary to note her thoughts, "That was during the revolt of the Maccabeem. Mattathias and his five sons led the people of old Palestine against the tyrannical power of Antiochus IV, ruler of the Greek-Syrian empire. In fact, the celebration of Hanukkah, the festival of lights, began with their triumph."

To raise her people from the grips of despair and to encourage them not to underestimate the power of a handful of people who put their minds together, she wrote, "The Banner of the Jew." The poem was published in the *Critic* and in the *American Hebrew*:

"...
Oh deem not dead that martial fire,
Say not the mystic flame is spent!
With Moses' law and David's lyre,
Your ancient strength remains unbent.
Let but Ezra rise anew,
To lift the Banner of the Jew!"

By reconnecting to the heroic history, she regained a sense of pride in her Jewish heritage and culture. Emma was looking to return to a usable past from which they could draw inspiration to proceed into the future. Her heart became as clear as crystal, and she understood how important roots were for a sense of identity.

"I have so many ideas, so much that I want to say. I just need more time," she thought. Emma often stayed up very late working and at times, even her fingers ached. She would change positions from sitting to standing, to kneeling; she couldn't stop. She poured her heart into her writing.

She used her pen as a sword that swung in two directions, to the non-Jewish world and to her Jewish community. Not only did she stand up for the Russian Jews and speak out against their oppression, she also appealed to the Jews themselves to step up and get involved, to make a difference.

She wrote, "We as Jews and as Americans, in these times, must keep our eyes on what really and truly matters.

We are obliged to stand and fight for what we know to be right. And that includes standing in the forefront of the fight against racism and anti-Semitism. We are counting on you. Please stand with us."

On another occasion, she wrote, "In this battle, and it is a fierce, dreadful battle, we most urgently and desperately need the help and commitment of each and every man and woman."

These words were the lifeline for the Jews struggling to survive the storms in Russia. It gave them new hope. They felt, after all, somebody cared and help was on the way.

Now that Emma was totally committed to serving her people, she became remarkably knowledgeable. In a letter to her good friend Rose Hawthorne, she wrote, "I am going to undertake the study of Hebrew in the fall... The Jewish question which I plunged into so recklessly and impulsively last spring has gradually absorbed more and more of my heart and mind... I have reached a point now where I *must* know Hebrew..."

Emma was so highly motivated that, in addition to Jewish history, she studied the Hebrew language as well. In less than a year, she knew enough Hebrew to be able to translate poems directly from ancient Hebrew originals.

She was very grateful to Dr. Gustav Gottheil, rabbi of Temple Emanuel of New York. "He is the one who first introduced me to the wealth of Jewish poetry. Through him, I discovered Jews were heirs of a spiritual fortune," she pondered. Now, she began to look for ways to recover these gifts of her people from the past.

She thought in her heart they would survive the present difficulties if they only could rise to their highest capabilities and regain confidence. They needed to renew themselves and build a life in the modern world.

She was inspired by the English writer, George Eliot, who believed Jews had to have a home, a Jewish state in their ancient homeland, Palestine. Emma realized not all European Jews could travel to the United States, although many did. Yet, they needed a better life.

Her ideas created an outrage because many people were opposed to them. Dr. Abram Isaccs, editor of the *Weekly Jewish Messenger*, wrote, "Any right-thinking person would be against it." Others were alarmed and said, "We don't have so much of a Jewish problem as we have an Emma Lazarus problem." She chose not to respond to these attacks and, instead, continued with her writing.

As she was getting ready to send her poems to the *American Hebrew*, she remembered another piece she had written. Immediately she added a note to the editor saying, "I've a play that I wrote a few years ago. It's based on an incident of medieval persecution of Jews in Germany that I think would be good to publish now in order to arouse sympathy and to emphasize the cruelty of the injustice done to our unhappy people..." The play she referred to was "The Dance of Death" which she'd kept in her desk drawer. Emma wanted very much for the play be published in a pamphlet in order to distribute it to as many people as possible at a very modest price. Philip Cowen, the editor of the *American Hebrew* was interested in her play. But, because of its length, he first printed it in his magazine in installments.

Later on, it was published along with Emma's new poems in a pamphlet. "What should I call it?" she wondered. After some thought, she came up with "Songs of a Semite." The pamphlets sold for twenty-five cents a copy, just as she'd hoped.

As her opinions became known all over the world, she was asked to speak in public gatherings. However, Emma didn't have the confidence to speak before large audiences. She wasn't shy though about speaking in small, informal groups.

When leaders of the community wanted her to make a presentation in front of big audiences, her reply was always the same, "I beg to say that anything in the nature of a lecture or an address is entirely beyond my province and capacity." Yet, she let it be known she would write the speech for someone else to read. In fact, she came up with a four-part plan to help with the emergency situation of European Jews. She wrote, "When we see a fierce fire burning, we must take action." Among the ideas she recommended were, "closer and wider study of Hebrew literature and history ... and a truer recognition of the large principles of religion, liberty and law upon which Judaism is founded and which should draw into harmonious unity Jews of every shade of opinion." She believed positive change must be rooted in traditional values and take its life from the eternal things, from the source of all life.

While she was caught up in her Jewish cause, busy and overworked, she still exchanged letters with Ellen, Emerson's daughter and her friend. Emma was very sad to learn Emerson's health was declining.

One day in April 1882, she received the bad news that Emerson had died. She wrote his daughter a letter:

"My dear Ellen, how much I thought of you and wondered how your brave and cheerful spirit was enduring the long, dreaded event. Yesterday I saw Tom ward who told me you were calm and well, and I write today simply to send you my most affectionate greetings and to say how constantly my heart has been with you and your dear mother."

## 17

## *She has a Mission*

*E*mma was greatly honored when asked by Ellen and her mother to commemorate Ralph Waldo Emerson. She titled her memorial essay "Emerson's Personality" and in June 1882, it appeared in the *Century*.

She praised his wisdom and goodness and went on to say, "nor is it too much to say that he was the inspirer and sustainer of countless heroes of some of the bravest deeds in our history."

Emma also brought out the notion that Emerson had "insisted on the moral element in art." She claimed, "For him, Shelley and Poe were distinctly not poets. On the other hand, ... very inferior, as well as, obscure writers might be exalted by him to a dizzy eminence ... simply because such writers struck or tried to strike that note of moral aspiration with which every chord of Emerson's great heart throbbed in unison."

That must have put to rest the question that had puzzled many of her friends who had often wondered why she stayed friends with Emerson. Hadn't he insulted her deeply by excluding her from his anthology?

Emma remembered the first visit to Concord when she'd hoped he'd bring up that sore topic. But he never mentioned it. Being as keen and sensitive an observer as she was, she understood his silence. Now, she revealed it. She wrote that unless Emerson had felt he could offer encouragement, he preferred "to disappoint them [the authors] by his silence rather than by his dispraise."

Later on, Emma learned, to her delight, that his family liked her article. In a letter to her friend Rose Hawthorne in September of that year, she wrote, "I found out after all what the Emersons' thought of my little paper on Mr. E. Ellen very kindly went over it word for word with my sister in order that she might repeat to me exactly the family opinion which was highly gratifying."

In the meantime, Emma read horrifying news coming from Europe and that many were fleeing the pogroms. It turned out that the more New York became America's world city, the more thousands of immigrants wanted to be here. They came from Russia and other oppressive countries.

Most of these refugees arrived penniless. Many families didn't come together. Often, a father or an older brother would arrive first to find a job and make some money. A few years later, they would bring over the rest of the family.

But many Americans thought these newcomers were troublemakers. "Don't let them in here, they are the scum of Europe," said those who wanted to stop immigration.

Emma, however, would shrug them away, "We all came from somewhere," she would say. "We are all immigrants."

"They'll spread disease," newspapers wrote to the alarm of their readers. Even the Jewish community gave a cold shoulder to the immigrants and called them "different Jews" because they were different in their dress, in their language and in their customs. They were an embarrassment for the local well-to-do Jews.

Emma decided to find out the truth about these refugees. She joined other committee members from the Hebrew Immigrant Aid Society and went down to meet with immigrants at Ward's Island in the East River. This was their way into America. Here the new arrivals were questioned, examined and tagged. They could be turned back for being too ill or too old. There was heartbreak and tears in this place, yet most made it.

"It was a hot, muggy day," Emma later wrote in her diary. "I saw people pushing, clutching, pulling apart, and twisting their arms, legs and bodies. Not understanding what was asked of them. Terrified men and women screaming and children crying, their eyes spoke of their suffering. They were tired, dirty, sick and sore. At first, I could hardly believe they were Jews. I'm used to Jews who are neat and well groomed, whose clothes were made of the finest fabrics and who live in nice homes."

She went on to describe how these refugees carried cardboard boxes, sacks or bundles all tied and knotted together with string. Women wore oversized jackets or men's coats and had their heads wrapped with shawls. Men had faded black or torn fur hats and big worn out shoes.

Emma later told Josephine, "When my eyes met the tired glint in their eyes, I no longer noticed their shabby and dirty outer appearances. Instead, I saw horrified human beings in great pain crying out for help."

When she went to bed that night after her visit at Ward's Island, she moved from side to side on her pillow almost as if to wipe out from her memory all that she'd seen during the day.

The next morning she woke at an early hour. As she bathed and dressed, she recalled crying out, "Ouch!" The pain came from her foot. Her injury happened when a woman, who'd been pushed, trod heavily on Emma's foot as she was leaving with the rest of the committee. "I can't get these people out of my mind," she thought. "I've got to do something. I must find ways to help or I'll not forgive myself for the rest of my life."

She made herself a cup of tea and sat down to drink. Her lips tightened, and her forehead furrowed with anger.

Then, Michael Heilprin's name came to mind and her face brightened. He was a Hebrew scholar who had fled from the persecutions in Poland at the age of nineteen. "I should talk to him," she thought. "My heart tells me that I ought to go back to these people. They're in such dire need."

Though many had cautioned her, "But, dear Emma, that's dangerous." She refused to listen. Her mind was made up and nothing would stop her. Michael Heilprin went along with her on many of these trips when she brought the poor immigrants money, food, clothing she had collected. She even gave them her own money.

Later she was horrified to see the brick tenements. Emma could not believe her eyes, how they all lived in small, cramped apartments. Not only did she meet Jews she hadn't known, she also discovered another kind of New York.

It had been said that New York was one city of sunshine and great wealth, and one city of shadow, a place of greatest poverty. She had no idea how true that was. She was shocked to learn there were two kinds of people in New York, the fortunate ones and the forgotten ones. The place they lived in was congested. Many windows were broken and patched with old newspapers. The conditions in these bursting slums were appalling, people sitting in pairs on fire escapes, others on doorsteps. Emma realized the only possession they had was the hope they'd brought with them in their souls.

Back home, as she picked up her pen to write a letter to the *American Hebrew*, a quick shaft of sunlight fell on her walnut desk. That made Emma think about the contrast between the brightness in her life and the darkness the immigrants must see when they have no one to turn to for help in their new land. She addressed the letter to Philip Cowen, the editor. When it was published, it created a stir in the Jewish community. The letter read, "The only appliances for washing consist of about a dozen tubs in the laundry and ten bathtubs in the lavatory. This was for seven hundred people. Not a drop of running water is to be found in dormitories or dinning halls, or in any of the other buildings, except in the kitchen. In all weather, those who desire to wash their hands or to fetch a cup of water, have to walk several hundred feet of irregular, dirty ground, covered with rubbish and refuse, and filled, after a rainfall, with stagnant pools of muddy water in which throngs of children are allowed to dabble at will…"

Emma felt these were courageous people who needed useful work to give them back their dignity. They would do what ever it took to survive because they had no home to return to if things didn't work out. Unfortunately, the reality was that most of them could not work. They simply had no marketable skills.

"I have this dream," she said to anybody who cared to listen, "I'm so certain, and so confident about it. I envision a technical school for those immigrants who do not speak English and have no trade or profession." Then she would go on to explain, "If they only had skills that were needed in the industrial world, I believe they could become productive members in the American society."

She organized meetings with leaders of the Jewish community to plan and raise funds, and she contributed her own money as well. On many such occasions, she would make silent donations, asking that her name not be revealed. As people began to pay attention to her, they became more and more interested in her ideas.

In one of her notes to Philip Cowen, editor of the *American Hebrew*, she invited him "to a very informal meeting at Dr. Gottheil's house for discussion of the eastern Jewish question." She went on to say, "I write with Dr. Gottheil's permission to beg you to be present, as I am especially interested in this subject. We shall not be more than a dozen altogether."

Soon her efforts paid off. The Hebrew Technical Institute was built and became a school for immigrant Jews. Many of its graduates went on to find jobs and begin a new life in America.

She also started an organization called the "Society for the Improvement and Colonization of East European Jews." Its purpose was to establish agricultural communities. Emma was of the opinion Jews could, and should, do various kinds of work including farming.

Her critics, on the other hand, often tried to dismiss this notion by saying, "A Jew cannot be an agriculturist."

That's why she was particularly thrilled when Michael Heilprin showed her a letter from a happy Russian immigrant, a farmer who'd settled in Texas. He wrote, "Our life is one unbroken paradise. We live a true brotherly life. Every evening after supper we take a seat under the mighty oak and sing our songs."

Then, one day, she had another bright idea. "These immigrants need to know the language of this country," she thought. Emma began saying, "Without English, they'll have little chance to improve their condition." As a result, shortly thereafter, she created special classes for immigrants to learn English.

By that time, the population in New York City had more than doubled to over a million people. It became increasingly difficult for poor people to find a place to live. That was another task Emma took on. Soon she was helping immigrants find housing in their overcrowded environment.

Although her outreach began with the plight of the Jewish poor, she expanded her concerns and embraced needy immigrants from all backgrounds and from every country.

For many of the newcomers, Emma was the answer to their prayers, and her soul, like an unshakeable rock, was their support.

Now she had so many demands on her time that she saw less and less of Charlie. Though this saddened her, she was determined to continue her mission to help the poor immigrants in New York City.

Throughout the 1870's, Emma had many of her poems and translations published in the nation's most distinguished magazines and newspapers. Yet, the years from 1880 to 1884 were her most creative and productive.

# 18

## Emma's Journeys

To help so many people and accomplish all the programs Emma had in mind required a lot of money. She began planning her next step. She could expand her efforts and go overseas to meet with the rich and famous of Europe and ask them to contribute to her causes. "A trip to London could be nice," she thought. "I've never been there before. It will be my chance to combine sightseeing with some fundraising. Come to think of it, why not?"

It seemed her friend, Rose Hawthorne, would be happy to join her. The more they discussed it, the more excited they became and began making plans. However, soon it was clear Rose had to back out because of trouble that had arisen in her family.

"I have to talk it over with Helena," Emma said to herself. As she loosened the clasp that held her hair in a bun, she pictured her friend. "She's such a good support to me. She so gently urges me on to spread my wings." Indeed, it was Helena who encouraged her to go ahead and go to Europe.

When Annie said, "I'll go with you." Emma burst with excitement. "You are my best friend in our enormous family!" As she said it, she noticed Annie's peach-like face full of smiles. "I'm in favor of going first to London," she didn't want to waste anymore time. She was ready to go. "The only trouble is," she went on, "Lady M. says everything is a great deal more expensive during the London 'season.'"

"If we find things too expensive after a week, we can leave and return later," said Annie.

"Right, I've said the exact same thing to Rose," Emma recalled. "We will change to another hotel or go to Paris or do something else."

One morning in May, both women jumped out of their beds with more than usual excitement. They got on board the Alaska and began their adventure. The ship was more like a floating town with marvelous interiors, glowing lamps and beautiful furnishings.

To her surprise, Emma didn't find the voyage nearly as dreadful as she had anticipated it would be. She thought she would be seasick the entire time. As it turned out, except for the first two days during which she slept solidly for forty-eight hours, she said she never felt better while at sea.

"I am enchanted," said Emma toward the end of the trip. "The sea and the sky seem to be cut out of a single sapphire."

Annie nodded and took it all in. "Ah, the sensation of land," she suddenly cried out.

After a week of ocean tossing, Emma was in a state of ecstasy. She kept saying, "It is a great event to be here." And then, over and over again, "I can hardly believe it is true."

Their first visit in England was to Chester where they spent four days. Emma enjoyed the walk around town.

"Look at that." She pointed at the old Norman wall with its gates and towers. "Isn't it unique? Look at the charming glimpses it gives into history and these queer, old winding streets how they are lined with houses."

"Shakespeare might have been born here, you know?" said Annie.

"I wouldn't be surprised. Oh, and look on the other side, over there."

"You mean the landscape?"

"Yes, it looks like green velvet. It's beautiful."

"In fact," said Annie, "every lane here is a picture, every house beautiful enough to be sketched or painted."

"Well, Annie, I promise that we'll allow special time for you to make a few sketches."

Standing on an old bridge one evening, they saw the Salvation Army marching along with drums and chanting hymns. Emma thought that it was exactly like a scene in a novel. She later wrote to Helena saying Chester was a fascinating little town, "and as we saw it with the rare advantage of bright sunshine and exquisite spring weather. We were quite beside ourselves with enthusiasm. When I tell that I attended services in the Cathedral twice, you can imagine how much I was impressed with the majesty and greatness of the Church of England... And, last Sunday evening at the service, Annie and I were rewarded for our piety by hearing an organ recital of the most classic kind on the glorious instrument... Here, in the Cathedral, I feel as if everything is very home-like and familiar to me."

Emma and her sister were simply overwhelmed by the grandeur and beauty that they saw there. But they had to move on to London.

"I wish we did not have to go to your Jews," said Annie as she glanced over with a smile to her older sister. Emma was thirty-four, ten years older than Annie.

"I know what you mean. It is difficult to leave a place like this. It's so lovely here," she acknowledged. "But then, we have a purpose, remember?"

She later wrote to Helena, "With difficulty we tore ourselves away for the goal of our pilgrimage, London."

On the way to the big city, she missed her friends back home. She wished she could share every nook and corner she had peered into with them. "I am happy as a queen," she said to herself. "This is all a dream, and a miracle, from beginning to end. It might have been even nicer," she thought for a moment, "if Charlie were here. He would've enjoyed it, especially the concerts." She recalled that when she'd left, he was coming down with a cold. By now she figured, it must be all cleared up.

Emma's trip to London turned out to be a great success. She was well-known particularly for her article "An Epistle to the Hebrews" that had made a strong impression there on Jews and non-Jews alike. And with her many letters of introduction, she was honored with receptions, dinner parties and meetings with those who shared her views regarding the restoration of a Jewish homeland in Palestine.

As she attempted to gather support for this idea, she wrote to Helena, "In London, my own people, the Jews, receive me with open arms ... The Montefiores, Goldsmids, Rothschilds, Moscheleses, Montalbas and a lot of others whose names you do not know." These families she mentioned were distinguished members of the British Jewish community.

She also met with George du Maurier, a well-known illustrator and satirist and with Scottish scholar and author, Andrew Lang. Among others, she saw James Russell Lowell, a poet and critic, who was U.S. Minister in London at the time.

"We saw a great variety of people in London," observed Annie. "What did you think of George Eliot's Mirah?"

"She is a very handsome Jewess. I wonder how George Eliot met her. To use her as a character in the book, *Daniel Deronda*, Eliot must have known her pretty well."

"I guess not many people know that George Eliot's real name is Marian Evans."

"I suppose not."

"Oh, Emma, that event on Friday, that we are going to..."

"What about it?"

"Should I arrange my hair the usual way?"

"Well, I think a new hairdo is a good idea."

"Have you thought about what you're going to say?"

"Not yet," said Emma.

"What do you suppose I should chat about?"

"I'm sure you'll think of something."

"That's easy for you to say."

Emma smiled.

Annie crunched her lips.

"What's the matter?"

"Nothing."

"Are we getting in to those 'nothing' answers again? I hate it when you do that."

"And you pick on everything I say," protested Annie.

"Don't be silly. Wouldn't you rather express your self in full sentences?" She put down the teacup she was holding.

"I like it better that way."

"Oh. Good reason."

"All right, then," said Annie. She picked up a book and settled herself in to read. A significant silence filled the room.

As Emma and Annie were going around town, the two were amused and entertained by what they saw, and their little ripple was quickly brushed aside and forgotten. They enjoyed the best concerts, theatre and opera.

Emma described it best when she wrote to Helena, "I rush from one variety of pleasure or interest to another and hardly know what I am doing... I have 'discovered' the National Gallery which I cannot get enough of, and Westminster Abbey. I can sincerely say the same thing about the House of Commons."

"I am bitterly disappointed," she wrote humorously, "in not seeing the slightest prospect of marrying Sir Moses Montefiore as I had hoped. He is approaching his 99th birthday and has not made any advances toward me and I fear there is no time to be lost." She liked to laugh about her spinsterhood especially since many of her friends and her brother Frank had gotten married and had families of their own.

Her two most special days in London were when she and Annie became good friends with Robert Browning after having been introduced to him by another friend.

"He is a famous poet," said Annie. "I can't believe he spent three hours with us at dinner."

"I know. I am living in a dream," sighed Emma.

"His stream of wit and anecdotes and poetry," said Annie. "It was all a lot of fun."

Emma mentioned he was a good friend of the Jews. "And I think this may be the secret of his immense kindness to you and me."

"I think so," agreed Annie.

"Look, he asked us to spend Saturday afternoon with him and his sisters. His older friends say he has never done that for them."

"Not only that," said Annie, "but he showed us his books and manuscripts, and his deceased wife's precious little souvenirs and treasures, and her Greek and Hebrew books."

"I hardly know what to say," said Emma, "except that we both had a most memorable time. And, I liked their lovely little house by the canal."

"He even gave you his photograph," said Annie.

"Yes, and what's more surprising, he wrote under it in Hebrew. Who would have guessed that? I was really touched."

But their greatest delight was meeting William Morris and getting to know the gentleness of his personality. They were both taken off their feet by his tenderness visible in every word, look and gesture. He invited them to his house on Sunday where they spent two captivating hours.

"Helena," Emma went on to write her confidant, "you would go simply wild in that house. It's just on the edge of the river, on a little avenue planted with magnificent oaks and looking out on a garden such as you have read about in the *Earthly Paradise*. The house itself is so different from everything else you have ever seen or imagined."

Jane Morris, his wife, was the beautiful model for many of Dante Gabriel Rossetti's paintings. And, Emma mentioned in her letter that, "Mrs. Morris is very beautiful and exactly like all the Rossetti pictures... She looks like an old, Italian portrait."

When they left, Emma kept on saying, "Didn't he look like a cross between an English sailor and a Scandinavian god?"

"Yes," said Annie, "especially in that blue shirt."

"And, look how he made us promise to visit him in August in his own home in Kelm Scott. Did you know it is said to be the loveliest house in England?"

Morris also took out a dozen maps and marked out a route for Emma and Annie writing down not only names of the towns and villages, but where to stop and where they should find the best stained glass and the best castles and churches.

On Friday, they went down to see his workshop in Merton Abbey. There he manufactured his beautiful textiles for his decorative art shop in London. His factory was a co-operative where the workers shared in the profits.

He told them, "I do not want art for the few, anymore than education for the few or freedom for the few." His dream was a just society. Emma admired the swatches of fabric and the beautiful colors he showed them. Both Annie and Emma were deeply impressed with this multi-talented man. He was a poet, designer, entrepreneur and socialist.

After that visit, she wrote to Helena, "Oh Helena, William Morris! I shall have a million things to tell you about him. Such a day we had with him down at Merton Abbey where his factory is. He is a saint and the only man I have ever seen who seems to be as good as Emerson. I don't know but that he is better, for he is more of a republican and not as much an aristocrat as Emerson was."

On Monday, they left England and arrived in Paris on July 14th, the anniversary of the Bastille Day. Right away they drove out in a carriage to Versailles where they spent all day. In the evening, the entire city was illuminated. It was indeed spectacular.

Emma described it in her diary. "The Place de Concorde was a mass of intertwined ribbons of fire, the bridges and river and arches were jeweled and outlined with the most brilliant flame. It was really like an enchantment, and I could not have believed it would be so beautiful..."

Yet, in spite of it all, Paris turned out to be a disappointment. Emma said to Annie, "Take away the Louvre and the art and I never wish to see this place again."

Annie agreed, "The ruins and decay make it difficult to walk the streets and squares. The buildings look like they were made of sugar candy, they are so white and filigreed."

"It is the most depressing place I have ever seen," said Emma. "I cannot imagine where people find the 'gaiety' of Paris and the good 'taste' of the Parisians."

"Even the cemeteries are in bad taste," Annie chuckled.

"Indeed, they cover the most sacred graves with wreaths of brass and wire that make even the dead ridiculous. Remember Heine's grave? Wasn't it pitiful?" Annie lowered her eyes and nodded in agreement.

"Well, I must stop being morbid. We better think of what we've enjoyed here."

"I can find a few things. How about these pictures of landscapes in the small gallery?"

"These are enough to drive you wild. And they have the best Rembrandt I have ever seen."

"And the show we went to, wasn't it funny?"

Emma laughed. "I cannot imagine anything finer, and I have to laugh to myself whenever I recall those scenes."

Nonetheless, she did not like Paris. She cut her stay short and did not stay for the entire two weeks as they had planned. Back in London, she received a letter from Helena that said Charlie was not well.

Emma wrote back, "I am very sorry to hear that your brother Charlie is not well again. I wish he could have come over for a sunbath in Venice. It would have done him more good than anything. Give him my kindest regards and tell him I don't agree with him on Europe!"

This time in London, with their friends and acquaintances away, they had a chance to spend more time at the National Gallery. Emma was especially taken by a Velasquez painting called, *Power of Prayer*. It was all in grays and pinks and blues.

Emma tapped lightly on Annie's shoulder and whispered, "Look at this little child in a light blue gown praying with the most divine expression on its face."

"Oh, it's extraordinarily beautiful."

They went to Surrey to meet with William Morris.

Again, Emma and Annie enjoyed his company and were very

impressed with his philosophy on life and art and his creative mind, as well as, by his most beautiful house and garden.

Emma's tour continued to Stratford and they went as far as Edinburgh in Scotland. Although she did not seem to write any poetry over that period of time, nonetheless, the letters she'd written about her travels were literary gems in their own right.

The last week in August she wrote to her friend Rose Hawthorne, "My trip to England has been one unclouded enjoyment. I am now thinking of our approaching return since we have only three weeks more in this wonderful country."

The last few days of their trip, Emma said to Annie, "I look dreadfully ugly and I have no clothes."

"I suppose you think you are the only one to feel that way." Annie looked at her and both had a hearty laugh.

When she was back home in New York, she felt as if she had grown ten years older since she'd started her journey.

# 19

## *A Mighty Woman*

*E*mma was glad to be home and enjoyed having dinner with her family. In fact, she had never been so happy. They were excited to see her, too. Her father was in high spirits and joking. After dinner was finished, their housekeeper cleared away the plates, a crust of bread, the peel of a fruit and empty glasses containing the dregs of tea. They all remained at the table discussing the trip.

"Travel today is much safer," said Mr. Lazarus.

"Oh, yes," said Annie.

"It's nothing like in earlier days when it was robber infested," said Emma. "Remember the stories Aunt Amelia used to tell us about how our ancestors got here?"

Josephine chuckled and said, "Oh, yes. That adventurous tale of how they arrived penniless."

There was a kind of suspense in the air, a stillness between conversations, something strange and new. It was as if something was changing, yet Emma did not know what it was. She felt a little impatient and was getting a bit antsy. She knew she had to get back to writing. She had her work cut out for her. There were several topics on her mind, some for articles, some for poems.

Emma continued working on her Jewish causes, as well as, on immigration in general and the arts. One day in November, her old friend, William Evarts, came over. He was the one who had spoken at the first protest meeting in Manhattan against the Pogroms in Russia. After some small talk, he said, "As you know, the people of France have given the United States this Statue."

Emma replied, "Yes, of course. If I'm not mistaken it is the work of the famous French sculptor, Auguste Bartholdi."

William continued, "Precisely. It is truly on an immense scale."

Emma's eyes widened. "That should be a feast for the eyes." She smiled.

"Yes, indeed. However, it requires a mighty base to hold it up."

"One can only imagine. Now, I remember reading Joseph Pulitzer's article. Has it been decided yet what to name the statue?" Emma asked.

"'Liberty Enlightening the World' is what they came up with," William said softly.

She liked the name. Emma also liked the fact that Liberty was a woman with a torch, lighting up the sky. William told her that the Pedestal Fund Committee decided to hold an art-loan exhibition and fundraising auction. Since Emma was a well-known and important poet, Senator Evarts, chairman of the exhibit, wanted a poem from her as well.

He mentioned those writers who were among the participants. The list was impressive: Longfellow, Whitman, Mark Twain, John Burroughs the naturalist and others.

"And we would like to include a poem by you."

"I have nothing I consider appropriate," Emma said.

"Then will you write something new for the occasion?" asked Evarts.

She was silent.

"It is a yes, then."

"Not really. I am not capable of writing to order," she said apologetically.

When he left, though, the Statue stirred her imagination. She pictured that mighty woman and how she mounts boldly into the sky with her light shining in the night. She was reminded of the immigrants and especially one Russian woman named Svietlana whom she had visited with her friend Michael Heilprin.

The first time Emma met Svietlana she had merely touched her hand and Svietlana started crying. She told Heilprin she was overwhelmed because, "Here is one of the well-groomed ladies who is simple and natural. I feel she understands what I am facing. I don't have to tell her."

When he translated it, Emma smiled and nodded.

"The look in her eyes is healing to my soul," she continued in Russian.

Emma was extremely pleased when she recalled Svietlana saying, "When she comes here, I feel I can breathe again. Then, I believe I am in America."

Behind her sweaty face and shabby clothes, Emma saw into the world from where she'd come, and felt Svietlana's dream for cleanliness, beauty and the opportunity to work and learn.

Now, she pictured the Statue holding the light further ahead to kindle the flame of hope, dreaming of better lives. She envisioned Liberty as the Universal Mother, making room for all her exiled children who needed a home.

Once she had this image, the words flowed quickly. She wrote with passion. Words, images, phrases and ideas rushed from her in an astounding flood. In one burst of inspiration, she wrote an immortal poem.

The New Colossus
Not like the brazen giant of Greek fame,
With conquering limbs from land to land;
Here at our sea-washed sunset gates shall stand
A mighty woman with a torch, whose flame
Is the imprisoned lightening, and her name
Mother of Exiles. From her beacon-hand
Glows worldwide welcome; her mild eyes command

The air-bridged harbor that twin cities frame.
"Keep ancient lands, your storied pomp!" cries she
With silent lips, "Give me your tired, your poor,
Your huddled masses yearning to breathe free,
The wretched refuse of your teeming shore.
Send these, the homeless, tempest-tost to me,
I lift my lamp beside the golden door."

At the bottom, she added the words, "Written in aid of Bartholdi Pedestal Fund 1883," and sent the Sonnet to the Committee.

The exhibit opened in December at the National Academy of Design on Fourth Avenue. The verses in the collection were read aloud, and the portfolio went for $1,500 to the highest bidder. The exhibition ran for four weeks and raised enough money to see the pedestal through its completion.

Soon the poet James Russell Lowell, then American Ambassador to England, wrote to her from London, "I liked your sonnet about the Statue much better than I like the Statue itself. But your sonnet gives its subject a 'raison d'etre' which it wanted before, quite as much as, it wanted a pedestal. You have set it on a noble one, saying admirably, just the right word to be said, an achievement more arduous than that of the sculptor."

Then she quickly forgot about it and became a busy Committee member, raising funds for the refugees and writing more articles, poems and letters. In one of her letters, she stated, "Dear Mr. Seligman, a meeting of the Society for East European Jews will take place at the Rice's house... May I beg that you be present without fail? I am anxious to have a full session as I shall present the report of my inquiries abroad and their result upon my own views. I think we shall then take action in regard to our future course. I am anxious that we should get to something practical with as little delay as possible..."

Her childhood friend, Minnie Biddle, and her husband, George, suddenly appeared in New York and dragged her away with them for the weekend to a charming neighborhood in Philadelphia named Chestnut Hill.

But as she described in a letter to Helena, "I have had a great fright about my father since I have been away from Home. He was taken suddenly and violently ill, and I packed my trunk to return immediately to New York when a reassuring telegram from my sister encouraged me to stay and told me the danger was over."

On Monday, Emma returned to New York. She had better news each day regarding her father, although, he was still sick and was attended by a nurse and a doctor.

## 20

## A Funeral and a Wedding

*M*arriage is a good idea," Emma thought. "Now, come to think of it, there was something so correct and pleasant in my parents' union that seems out of reach for me. Maybe it's because of my disposition. Poor papa, he must be missing mother so much."

In the morning, the nurse was alarmed when she saw Mr. Lazarus had taken a turn for the worse. He suffered all day with acute pain as well as weakness. When Dr. Draper came, he prescribed anodynes to alleviate his suffering. "He gave us no hope whatsoever," Emma told Josephine as she held her arms crossed over her chest.

Josephine nodded, sighed and finally said, "That's all we have to look forward to, his suffering and death."

Moses had great trouble drawing in air; each breath became more and more difficult. He felt some kind of pressure on his lungs and that caused him to hiss. Emma sat on a chair near his bed. Seeing the pain reflected in his eyes, made her want to cry. She recalled what a good father he'd been to them; how he took pride in her. She remembered the time he'd collected her early poems into a book. Her eyes became moist. It was painful to see him as he was growing weaker.

"I shove off the thought of the inevitable as much as possible," she wrote to Helena, "knowing that I shall need all the strength to bear it when it comes."

At night, she looked out the window as if searching for a star that could not be seen through the clouds. "I wanted to be out in the evening for my daily walk," she said.

"Under that timid sky?" asked Josephine.

"Yes. Before the darkness took hold. You know how I sometimes take walks to put the day behind me."

"I know," Josephine agreed, "that's sort of your way to prepare yourself for the night."

"I wish Papa and all else I care about would stay forever."

"So do I, except nothing is forever."

"I ought to have cherished more the good times as they were happening."

"Everything is changing so fast, it's so strange."

Emma sat in silence, lost in her own thoughts. "Everybody is like a flower that withers after being in full bloom," she sighed painfully.

Then one evening, Emma felt in her heart her father's love for her. It was different from the way she'd ever felt before. It was a pleasant, warm feeling that filled her inside and sort of embraced her. It was March 9, 1885, when Moses Lazarus died. Even though she'd been prepared for it, the loss was still very difficult for Emma to bear. "I've known many valleys between a few peak moments," she thought.

After the mourning period was over, she began planning a trip to London hoping it would cheer her up. But first she had to respond to the lovely sympathy note she'd received from Rose Hawthorne. She liked her so much and wanted to see her.

In her letter she wrote, "I am at home almost anytime, morning or afternoon. Come in the morning if you can. I am very well and busy enough with stupid little preparations for my journey not to have time for brooding or even thinking too much. Our experiences seem to be all pain, and I do not allow my mind to dwell on it."

Mornings were the worst especially getting out of bed because her limbs felt heavy without strength or desire to do anything. She was depressed. Yet, somehow, she mustered enough energy to get away. On May 16, she and Annie sailed to London. Emma hoped the trip would pull her out of the grief she now felt with the loss of her father. The plan was to visit England, Holland, France and Italy. They would be gone a long time.

As they steamed away from the dock, Emma saw Charlie in the distance. "It is very, very kind of him to come and see us off," she thought.

When they reached Chester, she wrote to Helena, "Here I am in England again feeling about twenty years older than when I was here last, trying with all my might and main to get back a healthy, natural way of looking at this beautiful world of ours. We are going on Monday to London.

I don't expect to see a soul in London. I can't say I wish to. So don't expect any interesting letters or exciting news. Tell the later [Julia] her slippers are the joy of my life. I use them every day. I forgot to say that my Harriet Martineau gown was the admiration of the whole ship! I wore it every day, I am taking it to London to be present in."

This time in London Emma and Annie's lives were quiet. For the month of August, they went to Yorkshire where they stayed in a country house in Richmond. Between resting and reading, Emma had time to think of the people she cared about that were back home.

"Tell your brother Charlie to write to me!" she wrote to Helena. She told her, with some pride, how she'd walked six miles in one afternoon. The weather was perfect with brilliant sunshine and that gave her the urge to be outdoors as much as possible. It was evident summer in the country helped her regain her health and vitality.

One day when she looked at Annie, then looked at herself, she smiled and said, "We walk about the whole neighborhood as if we owned it."

Annie laughed, "You mean we wear our oldest and shabbiest of clothes?"

Emma chuckled. "Yes, never meeting a soul and enjoying absolute independence. I have never had such perfect freedom and quiet in my life."

"Me neither."

"I hate the very thought of giving it all up."

In her next letter to Helena, she said, "Tell Julia her slippers are the stuff of life. As you can possibly see, my spirits have been much better since I have been in this lovely spot. Such beauty and peace are very great refreshment."

In the past, Helena had recommended that she read Tolstoy's great novel, *Anna Karenina*. However, Emma was frustrated that it was not available in the bookshops in England. "The English seem so stupid about any literature outside of their own," she told Annie. "I suppose it will take another generation to wake up to Tolstoy."

"It's a good thing," said Annie, "that on our last trip we introduced our friends to Turgeniev."

Emma smiled and nodded her head. "Now we are surrounded by his books; I'll tell him that when I see him in Paris." But first, they wanted to spend another week in London and from there, they would be headed to Holland.

In Hague, they enjoyed walking the streets along the canals to the other end of town. Along the way, they saw the house of the famous philosopher, Spinoza. As they came out of the picture gallery, they were surprised to find the streets swarming with crowds of people. It was the first day Parliament was back in session and they were waiting to see the King.

Emma was fascinated and wrote to Helena, "just like a scene on stage, came prancing first the richly uniformed trumpeters on horseback, then the court carriages with scarlet velvet trappings and gold decoration, and then in a coach all crystal and gold, drawn by eight magnificent horses, surrounded by a long guard, the king of Holland, a gray-bearded, old man bowing to his people. On top of the carriage was a huge gold crown placed on a crimson velvet cushion. As I had never before seen a king in my life, off a playing-card or the stage, you may imagine how full of interest and excitement the whole thing was..."

After viewing the pageantry of the king's parade, Emma and Annie went to the beach where the water had, "just about every color of the peacock," as Emma put it. They were impressed by the long line of fishing boats that stood out against the silver sky. The peasants, with their caps and fishing baskets in their hands, added to the charm.

Then Agnes joined them, and the three went to Paris. This time Emma was delighted, "I am in no haste to leave," she said. "I haven't had a moment of loneliness here."

Henry James, the famous author, was in Paris at the time, and came to visit her occasionally. She commented, "He looks well but no longer young."

"I thought so, too," said Agnes.

The last week in November she wrote to the Gilders to congratulate them on their new baby and, among other things, she told them that within a little more than a week, she hoped to be in Italy. Emma went on to say, "I have a letter of introduction to Mistral, but I feel so shy and unequal seeing people, that I don't expect to deliver it. I live in complete solitude animated only by my sisters and the great pictures and books of the world. I see men and women in the street passing like amusing sorts of phantoms, but they have no real existence for me; the only trouble with this life ... that I shall soon be unfit to speak to anyone. Fortunately for me I care a good deal for my old friends and when I think of you and Helena, I become almost human again..."

When she came to Pisa in December, she said she was drunk with all the beauty there. After three day in Florence, she was almost sick from all the excitement. She over did it trying to take everything in but particularly the artists like Leonardo, Michael Angelo and so many others. She collapsed and had to send for a doctor who, fortunately, happened to be a nice American young man with a good sense of humor.

"I have police officers," he said, "stationed at various palaces and picture galleries to keep my patients out of them."

To which Emma replied, "It is all very well for you who have been here for years to take things calmly, but what did you do when you first got here?"

"Oh," he said, "I made a fool of myself then!"

"So, it does seem inevitable," she replied.

Emma found Florence "more bewitching each day," and she began to dread the time when she would have to leave. Nonetheless, she had to tear herself away and leave for Rome.

Shortly after their arrival in Rome, Agnes had a sever attack of bronchitis, but fortunately, soon recovered. Rome made Emma feel like flying from one gallery to the next, "how lovely, lovely, lovely the Botticelli, Titian..." She went from one artist to the next not believing how beautiful their work was.

In her letter to Helena, she wrote, "I have the usual infatuation for the Italians and am willing to give 'my last franc for one of their smiles!'" She fell in love with Italy.

One day she turned to Annie and said, "There is so much to stay here for and so little to go home for, why don't we stay for another winter?"

"Actually, why not?" agreed Annie.

It didn't take long to decide. Emma began to immerse herself in the surrounding culture. She followed Italian politics, read Italian books and even began learning to speak the language. All of which gave her new interests and helped her forget the grief she was feeling after her father's death.

In April 1886, she wrote to Helena, "I heard that your brother, Charlie, was coming abroad this month. Is it true? It should be such a pleasure if he turned up in Venice. We are going there next week on the 16th and hope to stay a month. I feel as if I have a great deal in store for me."

But Charlie did not come to Venice. In May, Emma and her sisters returned to London. By that time, Henry James was also there, and he came to visit them. Her spirits were lifted and she was ready to see her other friends as well. It was end of May, when she was pleasantly surprised one day by Charlie finally coming to London.

"Looking the picture of health and good humor," Emma entered in her diary, "I was glad to see him, and in such full enjoyment of everything around him. He shared our miserable lodging-house dinner with us, and we exchanged our traveling experiences and it was quite refreshing to see him in such spirits." Charlie didn't stay long in London though he was on his way to Holland and from there to Italy.

In June, the rest of the Lazarus' arrived and Emma was very preoccupied with her family. Among them were her brother, Frank with his wife and two children, whom Emma was extremely happy to see. There was plenty of excitement. After all, Agnes was getting married to Montague Marks. He was Editor of the popular *Art Amateur* magazine. His father, David Marks, was the first Reform Jewish rabbi in England. And, he was rabbi at the West London Synagogue where Agnes and Montague were married on June 17, 1886.

Seeing her sister under the huppah (the marriage canopy), she thought Agnes was making the right choice. Anyone could see the bride and groom were perfect for each other. His eyes sparkled with joy, her eyes blurring with loving thoughts next to the glowing candles. The white dress, the cup of wine, it was solemn but very beautiful. The ceremony ended with the breaking of a glass under foot by the bridegroom to commemorate the destruction of the Temple in Jerusalem some thousands of years ago.

After the wedding meal, seven benedictions were recited, the most beloved of which was, "Soon may there be heard in the cities of Judah and in the streets of Jerusalem, the voice of joy and gladness, the voice of the bridegroom and the voice of the bride."

One of the few guests that Emma had invited, besides the two families, was Robert Browning, the poet she had met on her first trip to England.

He told Emma, "I've never been to a Jewish wedding before. The services were the most beautiful I have ever seen."

She noticed he seemed very moved by the whole ceremony. "Thank you for coming," she said. "We are glad to have a simple and solemn wedding and only wish all our friends would have been with us."

Josephine, though, wasn't doing well in London. From Emma's letter to Helena, it appeared that, "She hasn't been well since she arrived, as London climate does not suit her." Moreover, Emma seemed to be disappointed to find her sister had very little interest in the things she cared for so much.

On the doctor's advice, Emma and Josephine went to spend the greater part of the summer in Malvern hoping the blue sky and open air of the country would have an invigorating effect on Josephine. Yet, in another letter she told Helena, "Josephine is so depressed and homesick (though you must not tell her I said so). Of course, her weak condition must have something to do with her lack of spirit and interest, but I can plainly see all this new world would never have been the revelation it has been to me. My own curiosity and interest are insatiable."

Clearly, the two sisters did not enjoy the same things. It appeared Emma had the agility to bounce back from her father's death and become herself again. She started making new, interesting friends. Nonetheless, her new friends did not replace the old ones like Helena, Rose, Tom and others. She wrote them all frequently. Her letters about her sister's wedding that described it so beautifully with many little details were some of their favorites. Everyone loved getting letters from Emma.

Emma, however, felt a little bit guilty for not writing any new poems or essays. "I don't do anything," she said to herself. "The mere thought of writing paralyzes me and overwhelms me with painful memories."

In the meantime, as Josephine regained her health, she and Emma crossed over to France. From there, they planned to go once more to Italy before heading back home in a year's time.

## 21

# The Relapse

While in France, Emma suffered a relapse. "Paris is bright, beautiful," she wrote, "but I shall never love it. ... I am ill, as you know my strength comes back very slowly, if at all. I spend my days and nights on my back, and I can't even write a letter. All my dreams of returning to Italy are dashed to the ground, and I don't believe we shall leave Paris till we go home which will probably be as early in the spring as we can make it."

After this letter to her friends, Helena and Richard Gilder, Annie took over the correspondence with Emma's friends. Emma no longer had the energy even to write a letter.

Emma was eating breakfast when she saw her doctor through the window hurrying to see her. He was wearing a dark suit and wasn't smiling. He stood in front of her bed, his face relaxed.

Emma smiled at him. "It's good to see you," she told him. "How are you?"

He sat down near her bed and turned his head toward her.

"I wish I were outside now," she said. "People don't know how lucky they are to be able to walk around, breathe and enjoy the sun."

"No one knows he's lucky until he becomes unlucky," the doctor said quietly. "That is the way the world is."

When he left, Emma lay in her bed and began to think about her eyes and how she was beginning to lose her sight now in her good eye as well. She remembered tomorrow was Tuesday and, in the morning, her eye doctor was supposed to examine her.

That evening Emma sat up and looked out the window at the people below. There were only a few minutes of sunlight left. She looked at Annie and noticed how nervous and agitated she seemed that day. "It must have been something the doctor had said earlier in the morning," Emma thought.

Emma sipped her tea, and she and Annie sat quietly for a while. Seeing the strange expression on Emma's face, Annie asked, "Is anything the matter?"

"I feel so old," Emma said. "I have changed so much."

Annie stroked Emma's forehead, listened and said nothing.

Emma spoke in a gentle voice; it was almost a caress. She felt so altogether different now from the way she had been.

"Exhaustion combined with sleeplessness is a rare torture," she said.

The few hours she managed to sleep were usually terminated at three or four in the morning when she stared up into the yawning darkness, wondering at the devastation taking place in her body and awaiting the dawn that usually permitted her a nap.

"As I watch my condition worsen, I feel a loss at every turn," she thought. "Life is slipping away at an accelerated speed. How I wish I could see my father again." That was a devastating loss, and Emma tried hard not to think about it. But in the stillness of the night, thoughts of him would creep in and make her eyes tear. She had reached that phase in her disease where all sense of hope had vanished. Even though the doctor wasn't certain whether Emma had cancer, he knew Emma's condition was serious and that Emma was very, very sick.

However, Emma's intellect appeared more brilliant than ever before. Between attacks of pain, she talked about music, art, poetry and all that was dear to her heart. She came to appreciate when

Emerson had said to her, "What lies behind us and what lies before us are tiny matters compared to what lies within us."

"This body cannot press down the soul," Emma thought all the while trying to cheer herself up.

She now learned to listen to the deeper rhythms of life. The beat of her heart had grown deeper, more active, and yet, more peaceful. In a letter Annie wrote to Helena, she said, "Emma holds her own wonderfully in spite of all her afflictions."

From the music box came a sudden passage from Bach. This sound pierced Emma's heart, and in a flood of swift recollections, she told Annie, "I think of all the joys I have known with you and Mary, Sarah, Josephine, Agnes and Frank and how you'd rushed through the house playing, the celebrations we had, the love we shared, my work and my poetry, the voices and agility of it all." And she was silent again. A deep gratitude welled over from deep inside her for the concern that her family and friends were expressing. Now she looked forward to letters even more than before, especially to those from the Gilders.

"Your letter arrived last evening," Annie wrote to Helena, "when she was tossing and groaning taking her anodyne for the night, but she had the lights brought at once and read every word with the greatest interest. So you see even at this distance you can make her forget her pain."

In spite of her condition, Emma surprised everyone with her eloquence. "It is hopelessness," she said with detached clarity, "that crushes the soul even more than the pain. When one is moving only from pain to pain, there isn't anything left to look forward to."

It was now clear that Emma must go home. She could no longer stay in Paris, yet the mere thought of sailing across the ocean made her shrink. Somehow she managed to regain enough strength to be able to undertake the voyage.

Before leaving, however, she dictated a letter to Helena saying, "You will find me very dreadfully changed.

I have no use of my eyes yet, and have to be written for and read to. Under those conditions, I do not allow myself to think of the excitement of going home and seeing you all again, but you may imagine how eagerly I look forward to it."

On July 23, one day after her 38th birthday, she boarded the *Gascagne* and sailed for home. It was a terrible voyage. The sea was extremely rough. Even the papers wrote about it. The entire ten days of the trip Emma lay flat on her back. Tossed and shaken by the waves, she recalled a verse from Robert Browning's poem.

"Held we fall to rise, are baffled to fight
Better,
Sleep to wake."

Between naps, she pictured Aunt Amelia's face, her favorite aunt, who had told her and her siblings the enchanting stories of her ancestors who had come by boat and were robbed along the way. Now she felt just like them, coming to New York stripped of her vigor and robbed of her health. She had hoped to build herself up and start all over again the way her ancestors had done. But that was not to be.

After her arrival home on Sunday July 31, Emma continued to weaken and, after a few months passed, Emma was unable to rally and regain her health. On the morning of November 19, 1887, Emma died. It was 11:00 o'clock in the morning. Just like the title of the only story she'd ever written, "The Eleventh Hour." In it, she celebrated American heroism and the grand possibilities rooted in the American culture where she believed "art and beauty must and will survive."

# *Afterword*

## *Poet Warrior and Prophet*

*S*even days later, November 26<sup>th</sup>, was the Jewish Sabbath and Emma was eulogized throughout the country. The day was dedicated to her memory and the study of her life and work. Community leaders and international literary figures memorialized her.

Robert Browning, with whom she had shared so much during their time together in England, wired a cablegram sending "admiration for the genius and love of my lamented friend."

Charles Dana said she had the courage and logic of a man. (In those days, that was a huge compliment.)

Poet John Greenleaf Whittier wrote, "The Semitic race has had no braver singer."

John Burroughs, who felt a personal bereavement in her death, said, "She was one of my best friends." He then proceeded to say, "I valued her not merely for her literary genius but for her sympathy and attraction as a person."

The *American Hebrew* in December 1887, devoted a special issue to Emma. Her friends and colleagues wrote glowingly of her on the front page of the magazine. Walt Whitman noted that she had, "A great, sweet, unusual nature."

The *London Jewish Chronicle* wrote that Emma was a Jewish celebrity when she died. Because of her secular Jewishness and her call for a Jewish homeland in Palestine, not everybody agreed with her. At the same time, however, Emma had become a driving force in the Jewish community, and many saw her as the greatest Jewish poet of the nineteenth century. At her death, disputes were set aside and all Jewish papers across the country mourned her. She was recognized by all who knew her, Jews and non-Jews alike, as a "soul dedicated to aiding the oppressed."

Emma passed away one year after the Statue of Liberty was unveiled. At that ceremony, her Sonnet, *The New Colossus*, was read, then put away and forgotten. Sixteen years later, Georgina Schuyler, an admirer of Emma's, rediscovered the poem. In 1903, she arranged to have it engraved on a bronze tablet and placed on a wall within the pedestal of the Statue of Liberty.

The *New York Times* covered the event, and in the *New York Tribune*, Emma Lazarus was characterized as "the most talented woman the Jewish race has produced in this century."

Emma's sisters did not praise her as glowingly as her colleagues did. Josephine wrote a memorial essay trying to make her look feminine the way she understood it. Only in recent years has it been discovered Emma wasn't a "withdrawn" spinster as Josephine colored her to be.

Annie, after she married and converted to Christianity, refused to grant permission to reprint Emma's Jewish poems and withheld her diaries, as well as, many of her letters.

In spite of these obstructions, Emma's spirit prevailed. Not only was she recognized as a poet and a warrior, but a visionary as well. It turned out she was right about resettling the Jewish homeland in Palestine. But nowhere was her clarity of purpose more notable than when she understood the implications of the grave sight of her beloved poet, Heine, located in France that was surrounded by rubbish.

"Poor Heine!" she wrote, "I stood last summer [1884] by the grave of this free songbird of the German forest. He lies in the stony heart of Paris amidst the hideous monuments decked with artificial wreaths of bead and wire that form the usual adornments of a French cemetery... As I saw the rubbish and wreck left by the work of human destruction, I could not but reflect with bitterness that the day had not yet dawned beyond the Rhine, when Germany, free from race-hatred and bigotry, is worthy and ready to receive her illustrious Semitic son."

The rest is history...

# Acknowledgments

For permission to publish poems, selections from articles and letter from Lazarus's manuscripts and from publications such as *American Hebrew* and the *Century*, I thank the American Jewish Historical Society, New York, NY. I gratefully acknowledge Bette Roth Young for uncovering Emma's letters, and permission from The Jewish publication Society for selections from Lazarus' correspondence from Mrs. Young's book, *Emma Lazarus in Her World and Letters*. I also thank Columbia University Press for the permission to publish selections from *Letters to Emma Lazarus,* ed. Ralph L. Rusk, 1939 and the New York Public Library for selections from *The Letters of Emma Lazarus*, 1868 -1889, ed. Schappes, Morris U., New York, New York Public Library, 1949.

Printed in the United States
23942LVS00001B/157-216

9 780975 480342

# BIBLIOGRAPHY

Lazarus, Emma. "Emerson's Personality," *Century* (February 1883): 454-455, American Jewish Historical Society, New York, NY.

Lazarus, Emma. "Russian Christianity Versus Modern Judaism," *Century* 1882. American Jewish Historical Society, New York, NY.

Lazarus, Emma. "Letter to editor" ( to Philip Cowen), *American Hebrew* 1882. American Jewish Historical Society, New York, NY.

Lazarus, Emma. *Poems and Translations.* American Jewish Historical Society, New York, NY.

Lazarus, Emma. *Admetus and Other* Poems. American Jewish Historical Society, New York, NY.

Lazarus, Josephine. *The Poems of Emma Lazarus.* American Jewish Historical Society, New York, NY.

Schappes, Morris U. *The Letters of Emma Lazarus, 1868-1885,* New York, New York Public Library, 1949.

Rusk, Ralph L. *Letters to Emma Lazarus in the Columbia University Library.* Columbia University Press, 1939.

Young, Bette Ross. *Emma Lazarus in Her World and Letters.* Philadelphia: The Jewish Publication Society, 1995.

Eliot, George. *Daniel Deronda.* New York: Penium Group, 1995.

Richardson, Robert D. *Emerson: The Mind on Fire.* Los Angeles: University of California Press, 1995.

Birmingham, Stephen. *The Grandees: America's Sephardic Elite.* New York: Harper and Row, 1971.

Schoener, Allon. *New York: An Illustrated History of the People.* New York: W. W. Norton, 1998.